Hg2|Miami

A Hedonist's guide to…
Miami

Written by Todd Obolsky

A Hedonist's guide to Miami

2nd Edition

Written by Todd Obolsky & Charles Froggatt

PUBLISHER – Tremayne Carew Pole

EDITING – Nick Clarke, Eleanor Rosamund Barraclough,
Neil Simpson, & Andrew Connolly
DESIGN – Nick Randall
MAPS – Richard Hale & Nick Randall
REPRO – Advantage Digital Print
PUBLISHER – Filmer Ltd

Photography courtesy of:
(for Shore Club, Sky Bar) Opposite TOC page, 57, 116 Morgans Hotel Group
page 11 Greater Miami Convention & Visitors Bureau;
(Chesterfield) page 39 South Beach Hotels Group
page 61, 119 Hotel Victor
page 61, 66, 96 The Villa by Barton G.
page 65 James Shearer/Zuma
page 69 Barton G.
(Meat Market) page 80 Lyall Aston
(Skyline) page 143, 151 Pedro Galvez
(B.E.D.) page 145 RolloFilm.com <http://RolloFilm.com>
page 157, 159 Robin Hill/Adrienne Arsht Center

Email – info@hg2.com
Website – www.hg2.com
Published in the United Kingdom in June 2011 by
Filmer Ltd
10th Floor, Newcombe House,
45 Notting Hill Gate, London W11 3LQ

ISBN – 978-1-905428-43-4

Shore Club

Hg2|Miami

How to…

A Hedonist's guide to Miami is broken down into easy-to-use sections: Sleep, Eat, Drink, Snack, Party, Culture, Shop, Play and Info. In each section you'll find detailed reviews and photographs. At the front of the book is an introduction to Miami and an overview map, followed by introductions to the main areas and more detailed maps. On each of these maps, the places we have featured are laid out by section, highlighted on the map with a symbol and a number. To find out about a particular place simply turn to the relevant section, where all entries are listed alphabetically. Alternatively, browse through a specific section (e.g. Eat) until you find a restaurant you like the look of. Surrounding your choice will be a coloured box – each colour refers to a particular area of the Miami. Simply turn to the relevant map to find the location.

Book your hotel on Hg2.com

We believe that the key to a great Miami break is choosing the right hotel. Our unique site now enables you to browse through our selection of hotels, using the interactive maps to give you a good feel for the area as well as the nearby restaurants, bars, sights, etc., before you book. Hg2 has formed partnerships with the hotels featured in our guide to bring them to readers at the lowest possible price. Our site now incorporates special offers from selected hotels, as well information on new openings.

The concept

Ever had the feeling, when in an exciting new city, that its excitements were eluding you? That its promise failed to be delivered because you lacked the keys to unlock it? That was exactly what happened to Hg2's founder, Tremayne Carew Pole, who, despite landing in Budapest equipped with all the big-name travel guides, ended up in a turgidly solemn restaurant when all he wanted was a cool locals' hangout. After a wasted weekend, he quit his job and moved to Prague to write the first Hg2 guide. That was back in 2004, and since then, Hg2 has gone on to publish 32 city guides globally, all with the same aim in mind: to offer independent, insiders' advice to intelligent, urbane travellers with a taste for fine design, good food, the perfect Martini, and a city's inside track. Our take on hedonism is not just about pedal-to-the-metal partying, but a respect for the finer things in life.

Unlike many other guidebooks, we pride ourselves on our independence and integrity. We eat in all the restaurants, drink in all the bars, and go wild in all the nightclubs – all totally incognito. We charge no-one for the privilege of appearing in the guide, refuse print advertising, and include every place at our own discretion. With teams of knowing, on-the-ground contacts, we cover all the scenes but the tourist trap scene – from the establishment to the underground, from bohemia to the plutocrats' playgrounds, from fetish to fashiony drag, and all the places between and beyond, including the commercial fun factories and the neighbourhood institutions. We then present our findings in a clean, logical layout and a photograph accompanying every review, to make your decision process a quick, and effective one, so you can just get amongst what suits you best. Even the books' design is discreet, so as to avoid the dreaded 'hapless tourist' look.

Updates

Hg2 has developed a network of journalists in each city to review the best new hotels, restaurants, bars, clubs, etc, and to keep track of the latest openings. To access our free updates as well as the digital content of each guide, simply log onto our website www.Hg2.com and register. We welcome your help. If you have any comments or recommendations, please feel free to email us at info@hg2.com.

Todd Obolsky

Your humble author is a guy who harbors vast and voracious appetites, both gastronomic and geographic. I've sampled puffin in Iceland (not recommended), sought out the elusive yellow kiwi (the fruit, that is) at Kiwi360 in New Zealand, crawled for *pa amb tomaquet* and *cola de toro tapas* (washed down with Jerez sherry) in Barcelona, and braved vicious crowds for the perfect Montreal smoked meat sandwich. When not in Miami, in flight or on the road, New York City is my home turf; its international micro-neighborhoods impart the illusion of travelling while standing still.

Despite an epidermal layer that refuses to tan, I've been an unofficial Miamian ever since I was a wee bairn. I once took my fashion cues from Miami Vice (the TV show – look it up). And no other Northerner would even think of donning a Number 13 Dolphins jersey (in deference to 80s/90s Hall of Fame quarterback Dan Marino and his spectacular head of hair). These days the buzz of Lincoln Road and the mojito in all its forms make me crazy for Miami.

Charles Froggatt

Charles has written for some of the world's leading publicaions covering an eclectic mix of economics, international sport and travel. He has spent over three years in Argentina working in and around Buenos Aires as a journalist and working in the polo industry. His experience working in South American cultures primed him to write Hg2 Miami. After a brief spell creating his own extreme sports television series he returned to Argentina to take on the Hg2 Buenos Aires guide. For the past four years Charlie has worked in sports business and was one of the key figures in organising Polo in the Park, a modernised event in central London that saw polo payed in the capital for the first time in 70 years. Following this success he set up the International Polo Academy which launched in Argentina in March 2010.

■ Miami

Miami, as the media portrays her, is a peacock. Brilliantly-hued, confident and slightly outlandish, she is the tropical vacation queen of the U.S. and the well-dressed belle of the ball. The faces of fashionistas and Latin American business-men are animated as they speak of her, longing to be warmed by her gaze and her heat, and envious of her life of designer shows, dusk-to-dawn club-hopping, elegant dinners and potent drinks with VVVIPs. No one wants to remember that when the lights are turned off and everyone goes home, she reverts to her 'real' self. She removes the showy plumage she attached earlier, and so stripped, the pea-hen is as drab as can be (the peacock, after all, is the male, and yes, cross-dressing is not a foreign concept here).

You've heard the phrase 'the town that never sleeps' a thousand times before, but this is the one time when you should take it seriously. Shops and restaurants stay open until eleven and beyond, and bars are open until the small hours. If it's night-clubs - open until noon! - luxury cars, magnificent boats and beautiful people with huge egos you crave, you have certainly come to the right place.

But if you were expecting Americana in all its glory, prepare to be disappointed; Miami is a place where you could quite happily get by without speaking a word of English. The city is a teeming mass of ethnic groups that create an eclectic Euro–Latin fusion, with the Latin component encompassing Puerto Ricans, Mexicans, Dominicans, Peruvians, Brazilians, Argentineans and of course Cubans (Latinos make up around two-thirds of the city population, and Cubans account for about half of that figure). And in fact, what many take to be Miami is actually an amal-gam of separate cities. Miami (of Downtown) and Miami Beach (from the glitzy reputation of South Beach) are two entirely different entities whose residents view each other with healthy scepticism. Miami Beach-goers believe Miamians to be lower-class, boring workaholics who pale beside their fire and glamour; Miam-

ians think of themselves as authentic strivers who live with integrity, and those who live on the island as silly (but richer) pretenders; the citizens of Coral Gables, meanwhile, largely stay out of the fray, cocooned in their mostly upscale, refined community of business folk and trophy wives worthy of a reality series.

Besides the stream of Cuban (and other) immigrants that have arrived in waves over the past fifty years, Miami's growth has also been shaped, in one way or another, by the effects of smuggling. Originally stemming from the Prohibition era when lax enforcement of the ban on liquor led to an influx of people, and the beachfront became home to gambling, drinking and licentiousness. However, it also led to a real estate boom in the 1920s, during which cities sprung up and building projects came together as investment flooded in. But this increase in land value was entirely artificial, and the movement was felled by the Great Florida Hurricane of 1926, the stock market crash of 1929 and the ensuing Great Depression.

But that's ancient history. Today, commercially, Miami means banking, and the city continues to develop its reputation as a financial centre and as a link that connects the U.S. with South America and the Caribbean. And international trade through MIA and the Port of Miami is crucial to the city's health. But as evidenced by the

11.6 million guests that spent more than $16.6 billion in the area in 2009, tourism remains one of Miami's top industries, as visitors come from all over the world to sample her sunshine, indulge in her exciting restaurants and party in some of her brightest nightspots.

Miami

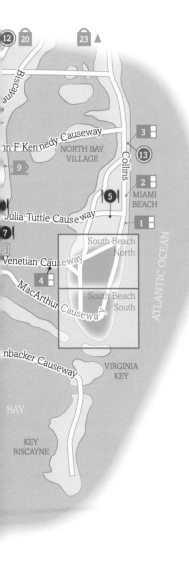

SLEEP

1. Circa 39
2. Eden Roc
3. Fontainebleau
4. The Standard

EAT

5. The Forge
6. Mercadito
7. Sugarcane
8. Versailles

SNACK

9. American Noodle Bar
10. Gigi
11. Morgans

PARTY

12. Dean's Gold
13. LIV
14. Magic City Casino
15. Tootsie's Cabaret

CULTURE

16. Adrienne Arsht Center for Performing Arts
17. Bay of Pigs Museum
18. Rubell Family Collection
19. Vizcaya Museum Gardens

SHOP

20. Aventura Mall
21. Coco Walk
22. Dolphin Mall
23. Bal Harbour Shops

South Beach *(North)* & Mid-Beach

Ocean Drive is all but a ghost town by 14th Street, and Washington Avenue has little value to the trendsetter up that way, either. So, it is Collins' responsibility to provide entertainment and distraction for Miami Beach's visitors. As it extends north past 14th Street, Collins becomes considerably less commercial. The few women's boutiques, accessory shops and trendy mini-chains give way to a smattering of smaller, cheaper hotels before meeting Lincoln Road and fully embracing the larger, more elegant properties such as the Ritz-Carlton and the Sagamore. The area almost whispers, "Give me your overly energised, your rich, your barely-clothed masses yearning to breathe dank air and pay $6 for a bottle of water in Clubland" like some sort of twisted Statue of Liberty. A handful of years ago, South Beach was characterised by Ocean Drive from 7th to 11th streets, where voyagers from all places would spend their time, drop their bills and hone their pick-up skills. But not any more, as any attentive 20-something knows, the spotlight is on Upper Collins and Lincoln now, and it's calling to them like a seductive siren's song.

Even in daylight, this is a stretch where you should always be looking stylish and chic. That way you can stroll into the Delano or the Gansevoort for a cocktail or late lunch without alerting hotel security. This is also the area where party palaces like Louis, Mynt, and Sky Bar emit their special signals – inaudible to responsible adult ears - that attract the glamorous, the extravagant and the sleek. The clubs are twilight worlds of fantasy, where time, lives and pension plans are lost. So, bring your AmEx platinum and plenty of stamina.

Further north is Mid Beach where the real people live. The mostly residential community offers miles of unspoiled beachfront and fewer logistical minefields (however, parking is a hassle no matter where you are). The grandeur of the Fontainebleau and Eden Roc, sprawling luxury mega-properties that have enough rooms to shelter a small city, are two good reasons you might want to venture so far out of the traditional comfort zone.

Back down, south of 15th Street, consider Española Way if you get tired of showmanship and are longing for some European charm. It's a crowded little gem of a street packed with unpretentious bars and restaurants and the feel of a Barcelonian plaza. Many of them (and just about all of the tourist-oriented shops) can be ignored, but some are popular with vino-seeking Spanish locals and can provide a modestly-priced, indolently enjoyable evening.

If Collins addresses the evening fantasies, everyday pleasures are handled by Lincoln Road, a sprawling pedestrian mall overflowing with just-opened restaurants, rowdy and refined bars, shops and galleries. On the pavement people-watching has become an art form. Here is where Italians would be practicing their passegiata and checking each other out if Miami Beach were transported to Sicily.

South Beach *(North)*

DRINK

19. The Abbey
20. Bar 721
21. Buck 15
22. Eno's Wine & Tapas Bar
23. Mova
24. Purdy Lounge
25. Rok Bar
26. Rose Bar (Delano)
27. Sky Bar (Shore Club)
28. Tequila Chicas

SNACK

29. A la Folie
30. Balans
31. Café Nuvó
32. Ice Box Café
33. Jerry's Famous Deli
34. Kung Fu Kitchen
35. Miss Yip Café
36. Pashas
37. Segafredo
38. Shake Shack
39. Tapas y Tintos
40. Tiramesu
41. Van Dyke Café

PARTY

42. Club Madonna
43. Louis
44. Mynt
45. Tantra
46. Score

CULTURE

47. Art Center
    South Florida
48. Bass Art Museum
49. Britto Central
50. Colony Theater
51. Fillmore Miami Beach at
    the Jackie Gleason Theater
52. Holocaust Memorial

■ South Beach *(South)*

Tell someone you're off to Miami, and they'll probably assume that you're heading for South Beach, or SoBe as label-loving locals refer to it. It's a magnet for hedonists, and without it Miami would not be known as the exciting city that it is today.

South Beach amounts to a small section of Miami Beach on a barrier island detached from the mainland, but it is, nevertheless, the heartbeat of the city. The Art Deco landscape is a product of the 1930s and 1940s, and was constructed after a hurricane demolished much of the beachfront city in 1926. The architects who rebuilt the community were given licence to create whatever they liked, and the result is an abundance of multicoloured, four-storey Art Deco landmarks.

More than 800 of these buildings survive on South Beach, partly due to the protection afforded by the National Register of Historic Places in 1979. Consequently, what you see is mostly authentic; any restorations undertaken on designated structures must be approved in advance and must not alter the original furnishings (in some cases, that means a hotel such as the Standard must make do with a neon Lido Beach Club sign instead of one of its own). However, the playful pastels that accent the façades of many properties were slapped on in the 1980s, dreamed up by Leonard Horowitz (see Art Deco in our Culture section). Similarly, the beach, like so many things in Miami, is cosmetically enhanced, bolstered by sand dredged from the sea-bed and dumped onto the shoreline. But who cares? The sand, edged

by turquoise water, provides a wonderful canvas for some of the prettiest sunbathers in the world.

If you want a clearer understanding of the place before you get here, just imagine the most louche and artificial arena possible and then fill it with beautiful people from all over the world who have come to party. If you go expecting culture and sophistication, then you'll be disappointed. Here money and fame rule, glamour and glitz are the order of the day and, as long as you accept that, then South Beach can be a lot of fun.

South Beach's geography is fairly simple: everywhere you'll ever need to go is strung along three parallel roads. Tourist-packed Ocean Drive is the Art Deco road set back from the beach, with a multitude of cafés and overpriced hotels. One block west is Collins Avenue, home to the glamorous and overstated elegance of some of Miami's finest hotels and boutiques. Finally, there is Washington Avenue: a grittier and edgier alternative to South Beach's playboy paradise.

Fifth Street is the main artery that handles traffic to and from Downtown Miami via the MacArthur Causeway; south of it lies a different South Beach, calmer and more residential. Surfers, an ultra-toned Latino crowd, and a few families populate the shore on this end. True Miami locals like to go here to escape the tourists; after some time in Miami's fast lane, you may want to as well.

South Beach (South)

SLEEP

1. Astor
2. The Bentley Hotel & Beach Club
3. Breakwater
4. Chesterfield Hotel
5. Clinton Hotel
6. The Hotel
7. The Mercury South Beach
8. Hotel Ocean
9. The Pelican
10. St. Augustine
11. The Savoy
12. The Victor
13. The Villa by Barton. G
14. Whitelaw Hotel

EAT

15. China Grill
16. De Rodriguez Ocean (Hilton)
17. Escopazzo
18. Joe's Stone Crab
19. La Locanda
20. Osteria del Teatro
21. Prime One Twelve
22. Shoji Sushi
23. Smith & Wollensky
24. Spiga
25. Taverna Opa
26. Wish (The Hotel)
27. The Villa by Barton G.

CULTURE

51. Wolfsonian-FIU
52. World Erotic Art Museum
53. Ziff Jewish Museum

DRINK

28. Automatic Slims
29. Club Deuce
30. Finnegan's Way
31. Jazid
32. Monty's
33. Palace
34. The Room
35. Safari Bar
36. Tiffany Spire
    Bar (The Hotel)
37. Vue/Passage Bar (Hotel Victor)

 SNACK

38. 11th Sreett Diner
39. Cardozo Café
40. Cavalier Crab Shack
41. David's Cafe
42. Joe's Take Out
43. News Cafe
44. Pelican Café
45. Le Sandwicherie

 PARTY

46. B.E.D.
47. Mansion
48. Nikki Beach
49. Skyline
50. Twist

 SHOP

▇ Collins Avenue
▇ Ocean Drive
▇ Washington Avenue

Downtown

Architecturally, Downtown Miami boasts one of the most impressive skylines in the United States, with rows of skyscrapers and the Four Seasons poking its polished tinted glass head above a bank of towers, all set against a backdrop of shimmering blue water. However, many would say that Downtown is best enjoyed from a distance. Indeed, it's not the shiny modern landscape that it appears to be. For long stretches it can seem like a ghost town, with a few lunchtime bars for workers and an array of electronic stores and downmarket shopping strips. Businessmen stay above ground level in their glistening corporate towers during office hours, then jump into the elevator to the subterranean car park and drive home to the suburbs when the working day is over. Even worse, if you take a wrong turn, you could find yourself in serious trouble (especially in the areas surrounding the elevated Dolphin Expressway, I-395 and I-95).

The area had been rejuvenated as investors pumped cash into the area in the few years before the onset of the recession. The catalyst for the facelift was the groundbreaking Adreinne Arsht Performing Arts Center (the largest performance complex in Florida and No. 2 in the U.S. in terms of area). Designed by Cesar Pelli, the Center makes an emotionally blinding impression and signalled a green light to the construction of a number of upscale apartments. The Downtown renaissance stalled, however, and the sound of change now rings as hollow as many of the unoccupied chambers in those multi-floored homes.

Miami proper, in area, is smaller than any other major U.S. city, but the Downtown district is nonetheless vast. There are a few areas, however, that are likely to pique your interest. The financial industry is largely located along Brickell Avenue, in a neighbourhood that maintains an air of seclusion, though it's far from private. The

Four Seasons and Mandarin Oriental call this stretch home, and are frequented by businessmen and women (on holiday and not) and the visitors trying to escape the mass liquoring up of South Beach. Somewhat northeast of there -– still on the mainland – is the Design District. Bordered by North Miami and NE 2nd avenues on the west and east, and NE 38th and NE 41st streets, here you'll find a high concentration of smart interior design and home furnishings shops, along with 26 galleries and a smattering of eateries. A more art-orientated development is in Wynwood, a bit south of the District and scattered along NW 2nd Ave and its off-shoots, mostly between NW 22nd and 28th streets. These latter two put on gallery nights and host events and spontaneous displays (refer to www.miamidesigndistrict.net and www.wynwood.com for much more detail).

In terms of nightlife, Downtown is where it's at. It's South Florida's answer to Ibiza, and home to the largest nightclubs for house and trance music in the state. Nocturnal and Space are superclubs that bring in top-name international DJs for their marathon sessions that last almost until the 9-to-5ers start shutting down the streets. The new Mekka is young, fun, large and loud. Downtown clubs, with 24-hour liquor licenses and warehouse spaces, provide a freedom and vague sense of danger that South Beach proper will never be able to duplicate.

Downtown

 SLEEP

1. Conrad Hotel
2. Epic Hotel
3. Four Seasons
4. Mandarin Oriental
5. The Viceroy

 EAT

6. Abokado
7. Azul (Mandarin Oriental)
8. Eos
9. The River Seafood
   & Oyster Bar
10. Zuma (Epic Hotel)

DRINK

11. Bahia (Four Seasons)
12. The Bar at Level 25
13. Gordon Biersch Brewery
14. M-Bar (Mandarin Oriental)
15. Transit Lounge

0   0.5   1km

 SNACK

16. Baru Urbano

 PARTY

17. Mekka
18. Nocturnal
19. Space

 CULTURE

20. Bay Front
    Park Ampitheatre

25

Coral Gables

Coral Gables, eight miles from Downtown and around twelve from 800 Collins Avenue, is very different from Miami's other suburban districts. Lush green parks and golf clubs are nestled between quiet streets that are lined by massive trees with overhanging branches in front of detached terracotta roofed houses. These are inhabited by the wealthy, which have the local Cubans (Little Havana just to the east) wash their cars and mow their lawns.

Hedonists may be disappointed by the fact that Coral Gables is a tranquil area and not a place for parties. It is telling that George Merrick designed it (along with his uncle and artist Denman Fink and landscaper Frank Button) in the 1920s in an effort to create the perfect environment to raise families in a planned community. With fountains and archways, informal city 'entrances' made of stone, plaza-like crossroads, streets named Ponce De Leon and Aragon, and Spanish hacienda architecture, they give Coral Gables – the safe, respectable neighbourhood of Miami – a truly European flavour. So, too, do the architecturally honest 'villages' dotted throughout the city. Italian, French and Dutch influences can be felt as well as a smattering of ornate Oriental architecture. Coral Way is the major artery for the twelve-square-miles that make up Coral Gables. Locally known as the Miracle Mile, it runs east-west and has its own half-mile stretch of boulevard packed with shops, businesses and restaurants.

So why trek over here? Although the majority of the neighbourhood is residential, Coral Gables is also host to almost 200 international firms, so if you are in town on business there is a good chance that you'll be spending some time here. For

shopping, there are little boutique stores of recognisable quality along Coral Way, as well as the Village of Merrick Park, an up-and-coming designer mall where that European influence is on display in the less showy windows and the more selective range of stores.

Most importantly, Coral Gables is considered the food capital of Florida and boasts some high-quality restaurants. Although they are not renowned for their atmosphere, in culinary terms they are generally superior to the restaurants on South Beach and Downtown. You may fancy heading over to Coral Gables for an early dinner at Talavera or Ortanique before returning to Downtown or South Beach for the bright lights.

Unless you have a particular fondness for sleepy suburbs, staying in Coral Gables probably won't be very tempting. Golfers, however, should not forget the Biltmore – which not only boasts an 18-hole golf course but also, until recently, the biggest hotel pool in the continental United States. The hotel's Fontana offers the possibility of a wonderful lunch among greenery and fountains in the middle of the day and a quiet dinner in the evening.

If South Beach's constant fashion parade gets just a little too much for you, an afternoon lounging by the pool at the Biltmore, followed by a little shopping at Merrick Village before a quiet dinner at La Cofradia might just save you.

Coral Gables

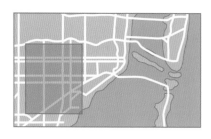

0   250   500m

 SLEEP

1. Biltmore

 EAT

2. Caffe Abbracci
3. La Cofradia
4. Norman's 180
5. Ortanique
6. Por Fin
7. Le Provencal
8. Talverna

 SNACK

9. Fontana
10. Patagonia

 CULTURE

11. Actors' Playhouse
  at the Miracle Theater

SHOP

12. Village of Merrick Park

29

Clinton Hotel

sleep...

In Miami your choice of accommodation is your calling card so it is worth forking out that little bit extra if you intend to look the part. Put simply, the amount you spend will determine how luxurious your bedroom is, how relaxing the hotel spa is, how big your swimming pool is, and, most importantly, how close to the beach you will be. Monetary concerns aside, making that decision is only as easy or hard as you make it. To simplify – what is it you want? If you envision long sessions slow-roasting yourself at the edge of the Atlantic, followed by hours of drinking, dining and debauchery, focus on location. If self-reflection and a spot of R&R is what you had in mind then match the hotel's underlying mood to yours. Perhaps your aim is to make your friends and the rest of the peninsula jealous of your taste in sports-wear, jewellery and bravado? Obviously, charisma and sophistication should be factored in. Luckily, we've done the work for you in this regard, as each of our selections is assessed relative to convenient location, style and atmosphere. Still too daunting? Don't worry – all the hotels listed here promise satisfaction. Guaranteed.

If you've chosen Miami as your destination, a cool pool will probably be high on your wish list. The beach is on every visitor's mind – to the point where it lacks originality. All of the big-budget hotels have luxurious pool areas, while some smaller boutique hotels, such as the Bentley or The Hotel, have iconic rooftop pools. There are some excellent lodgings – for example, the Townhouse – that do not have pools but do have access to the pools of other hotels.

Only a very good hotel would draw you away from South Beach or Miami proper. The Biltmore Hotel is the jewel in Coral Gables' crown – and therefore, the only one we included. This grand, luxurious old hotel should not be overlooked. If not for a room, consider a luxurious dinner, or a snack on the edge of its stellar pool. Golf provides another reason to stop by, since the property's championship 18-hole course offers a real challenge to even the most seasoned swinger.

If SoBe's scene of glitter and grease is not a main concern, Downtown is an increasingly convincing draw. Businessmen usually look no further than the Four Seasons or the Conrad, two boastfully showy choices that can handle even the pickiest tycoon. Then there is the Mandarin Oriental, a luxurious oasis on Brickell Key that overlooks the city's twinkling skyline. A number of new options have also sprung up during the past few years. Tower complexes can provide the best of a hotel visit but in a residential setting. Condos lie above, below or across the courtyard from guest rooms, and with the addition of a posh restaurant and/or spa, guests don't feel compelled to leave the property. The Epic and the Viceroy are two such establishments, the latter with a much talked-about restaurant, the former with an expansive rooftop pool area and lounge (with fireplace). In any case, several clubs and noteworthy restaurants have set up stakes in Downtown and in the Design District of late, so a night out need not involve driving over a bridge.

There are a number of interesting options at the other end of the scale, too. More popular than ever are those low-profile places that manage to be both affordable and possess that down-market chic; a double bonus for those who aren't particularly rich or famous but want to keep that information hidden. So, keep this on the down-low: value, in the form of comfortable stylish surroundings in contrast to the level of room rates, can be won at the Whitelaw, Catalina, Savoy, Townhouse, and Circa 39.

The rates quoted here are for a standard double in low season and a one-bedroom suite in high season.

sleep…

the best hotels…

Our favourites:
Biltmore
Fontainebleau
The Hotel
National
Pelican
The Raleigh
Sagamore
The Setai
Shore Club
The Villa by Barton G

For Style:
National
Pelican
Sagamore
The Setai
The Villa by Barton G.

For Atmosphere:
Fontainebleau
Mandarin Oriental
TheRaleigh
The Setai
The Villa by Barton G

For Location:
Catalina
Delano
Ritz-Carlton
The Hotel
Whitelaw

The Astor (left)
956 Washington (10th St) Avenue, South Beach
Tel: 305 531 8081
www.hotelastor.com
Rates: $120–750

One of Washington Avenue's top properties (along with Hotel Clinton), the Astor was designed by architect T. Hunter Henderson in 1936 and renovated to dispassionate effect in 2002. The hotel's neatly kept hedgerow and small garden in front of the building's coral stone façade project gentility. Astor's 40 rooms, standard for a building of this period, are inviting with blond oak wood beds dressed in Frette linens and offset by chrome accents and splashes of cool green and soothing lilac. The worthy in-house restaurant, D. Rodriguez Cuba, spotlights the country in the form of elevated traditional recipes and offers, for those so inclined, a comfortable patio on which to puff cigars. You may want to take advantage of one of the packages offered – they include dinner, a day on a boat, and bottles of wine or vodka – (good value in a landscape where deals are few and far between).

Style 8, Atmosphere 8, Location 7

Bentley Hotel (right)
& Beach Club
510 Ocean Drive (5th St), South Beach
Tel: 305 538 1700
www.thebentleyhotel.com
Rates: $175–1,200

The Bentley plays it cool, preferring to focus on its guests than beating its name into the Miami consciousness. Sitting a couple of doors down from the anything-but-quiet TGI Friday's (one of the two chain establishments on the strip), the Bentley is an attractive option for a weekend away. The rooftop pool and Jacuzzi have uninterrupted views of the beach, the hotel has a (rare) dedicated area of the sand a couple of blocks south, and the Bentley performs in the bedroom with elevated platform beds. Plus, every room is a suite and each comes with a sitting area and an equipped kitchen or kitchenette (the better to avoid the hawkers on the Drive). Indeed, this hotel attracts the kind of client that has a substantial amount of cash in the bank but does not feel the need to tell the world about it, and thus adds a touch of class to otherwise flashy Ocean Drive.

Style 8, Atmosphere 7, Location 8

Betsy (bottom)
1440 Ocean Drive (14th Pl), South Beach
Tel: 305 531 6100
www.thebetsyhotel.com
Rates: $290–700

Like the Raleigh, this hotel looks much as it did when it was opened as the Betsy Ross Hotel in 1942, and is quite happy to evoke the city's humble 'teenage' years (minus the associations of war and rationing). The lobby is dressed in 'upscale plantation', properly reflecting the Georgian colonial façade - a unique example on this strip - but it was in fact designed by the father of Miami Art Deco, L. Murray Dixon, in a departure from his usual work. In any case, what you'll find in the guest quarters today are custom poster beds clad in Frette linens, black walnut flooring, and airy marble bathrooms with plenty of light and mirrors. The colour scheme is full of restful ivory, cream and tan, with lilac and pastel green accents to ensure you aren't lulled to sleep too early. The Betsy is clearly for seekers of solitude. Its location at the upper end of Ocean Drive, where the residential district laws are strictly anti-noise, means you can retire at 9pm if you desire. The hotel's dining option is BLT Steak, an entry in the capable-chef-blows-up sweepstakes that is reliable, if pricey.

Style 8, Atmosphere 7, Location 7

....

Biltmore *(top)*
1200 Anastasia Avenue (Columbus), Coral Gables
Tel: 305 445 1926
www.biltmorehotel.com
Rates: $180–1,850

Way before the heyday of the Fontainebleau, the Biltmore was an established entity in Coral Gables. The baby of city founder/land developer John Merrick, hotel guru John McEntee Bowman and architect Leonard Schultze (who created Grand Central Terminal in New York), the $10-million Biltmore opened in 1926. Over the next two decades, the likes of Judy Garland, US President Franklin D. Roosevelt and Chicago gangster Al Capone lounged around in their bathing clothes on the banks of the 23,000-square-foot pool. Now it is a historic landmark after the city of Coral Gables took over the property, re-opening it in 1987 after a $55-million refurbishment before handing it over to a private company. The Biltmore is the go-to spot for those travellers less captivated by clubbing and more interested in serious shopping and golfing. The hotel owes much to Spain, as the bell tower was modelled after Seville's Giralda, and the multitude of columns, courtyards and glazed tiles is reminiscent of Córdoba's Mezquita. Indeed, your first walk through the lobby will take your breath away with its hand-painted vaulted ceilings, 25-foot columns, enormous bird-cases filled with brilliantly-hued finches, porcelain planters, French and Spanish furniture and floors clad with marble and Oriental rugs.

Style 9, Atmosphere 8, Location 5

....

Breakwater *(bottom)*
940 Ocean Drive (10th St),
South Beach
Tel: 305 532 2362
www.breakwatersouthbeach.com
Rates: $300–810

After a period of hibernation, the Hotel Breakwater (with a rich history dating to 1939) recently woke up after a crisp reno by the Jordache organization. Now joined to the adjacent (former) Hotel Edison, it's the biggest opening in South Beach in quite some time, with 99 king bed rooms sporting the necessary gadgets, private terraces and rainforest showers (and another prized feature – soundproofed windows). In one of its previous lives, the hotel's rooftop served as the setting for a provoca-

tive ad for Calvin Klein jeans featuring Brooke Shields. But for now guests can check out the swanky rooftop lounge Intimissimi in the evening, or the Wellness Garden (with the glass-enclosed pool) in the daylight hours. The Breakwater is boutique, but not stuffy; energetic, but not fakely so.

Style 8, Atmosphere 8, Location 8

Catalina *(top)*
1732 Collins Avenue (18th St),
South Beach
Tel: 305 674 1160
www.catalinasouthbeach.com
Rates: $90–399

The Catalina is a bit of an anomaly in South Beach in that it markets itself to a decidedly youngish, budget-conscious crowd. Not that you'd be able to tell from the sleek white piano in the lobby or the busy Red Bar populated with hipster music types. The property's official name is the Catalina Hotel and Beach Club, as it boasts both ground level and rooftop pools, and provides free beach loungers for a day on the sand across Collins Avenue. Located on the 'lesser' hotel side of Collins Avenue, the Catalina can be identified by its large windowed front that looks like a sports-car showroom. The lobby and the rooms are dressed in a tranquil white with occasional bright accents, and rooms range from 'It's a Small World' (miniscule, with rate to match) to 'South Beach Rock Star' and 'El Grande.' Visitors can enjoy the three bars, two restaurants (Kung Fu Kitchen & Sushi and Maxine's) and complimentary VIP club

passes. But remember to plan your day wisely: Red Bar serves free drinks to hotel guests between 7 and 8pm.

Style 8, Atmosphere 9, Location 9

Chesterfield Hotel *(bottom)*
855 Collins Avenue (9th St),
South Beach
Tel: 305 531 5831
www.thechesterfieldhotel.com
Rates: $100–370

The Chesterfield was recently updated and extended across three buildings (incorporating the adjacent Lily and Leon). So, where young professionals and long-legged models once loitered in slightly cramped surroundings, they now have room to roam. It's fairly popular, though pool-less, and the rooms, rendered in aluminium and mahogany, are well equipped. Luxurious is not quite the word for the Chesterfield, but its black-and-white based post-Depression-style lobby – though compact – does exude that impression. Visitors during the day should take a breakfast coffee and muffin onto the open porch to avoid the stampede of arriving and departing guests. As dusk falls, guests should take advantage of the fun Safari Bar and sit under stuffed animal heads. Like the Catalina and Whitelaw in the South Beach Group, guests enjoy free drinks for an hour in the evenings, as well as free rides to and from the airport and the deal-clinching potential of skateboard and scooter rentals.

Style 7, Atmosphere 7/8, Location 8

Circa 39
(top)

*3900 Collins Avenue (39th St),
Mid-Beach
Tel: 305 538 4900
www.circa39.com
Rates: $100–260*

'Mid-Beach' is Circa 39's noticeably residential neighbourhood home, which means that the hotel is removed from the hysteria of South Beach proper (a plus or a minus, depending on your mindset). The focus this far north is definitely on the beach as citizens of all stripes set out early, bake for hours, before returning to their dens late in the afternoon to gear up for a night of drinking elsewhere, or for calmer contemplation. Circa 39's rates are satisfyingly low for an establishment that offers 100 decently-sized rooms (this is a classic Art Deco building so all rooms are similarly sized) in two buildings, decorated in soothing pale blue and white, a large pool with massage cabanas, in-room WiFi, and Play, a stylish bar that is fairly popular with Miami's in-crowd. Circa 39 exudes a positive energy without the Miami-standard pretension. Take your provided chairs and towels to the beach a minute's walk away, pick your spot on the acres of free sand, and think how content you are away from the teeming masses twenty blocks south.

Style 7, Atmosphere 8, Location 7

. . . .

Clinton Hotel
(bottom)

*825 Washington Ave
(8th St), South Beach
Tel: 305 538 1471
www.clintonsouthbeach.com*

Rates: $240–500

The cheeky giant plush 'lamp' with seating around its base in the lobby has sadly departed, but the Clinton's still got its sense of humour. Just look at the wading pool courtyard deck, which changes its striking clothes with the season for evidence (now dressed in lime green, replacing the prior raspberry-hued motif). Newly opened in 2004, the Clinton is as boutique as they come; the Art Deco façade looks a bit stolid, but the new interior is designed with high-spirited style. Some of the 82 rooms have mini verandas that overlook an enclosed ankle-deep ornamental pool, unique in Miami, while others watch over the courtyard area. The bathrooms all have large windows looking into the bedrooms over the basins so that lovers need not lose eye contact while they floss. If you're in one of the six suites, your spa tub resides on the balcony, and 'bath butler' services are available (though presumably they only draw the bath and don't actually get in with you). More service-orientated than many of the mid-level South Beach lodgings, the hotel also offers 24-hour concierge service, guaranteed entry to all Miami nightclubs, a full-service spa and fitness centre, and WiFi throughout. If you are a shopaholic, like to party and don't mind a small pool, then the Clinton is the place to be.

Style 8, Atmosphere 7, Location 7

. . . .

41

Conrad Miami *(left)*
1395 Brickell Avenue
(SE 14th St), Downtown
Tel: 305 503 6500
www.conradmiami.com
Rates: $170–600

The Espirito Santo Plaza building, a 36-storey structure built of concave glass, is unquestionably the sexiest building in the Downtown area. The Conrad Miami, housed inside it, is every bit as seductive, first thrilling guests with its 25th-floor Sky Lobby and its eleven-level atrium, then with the spectacular views afforded from the Bar. With its shiny lemon barstools, high-backed open booths and daily bar specials, it is the cream of the Downtown hotel bar scene. The 203 rooms represent a harmonious mix of contrasting elements of glass, wood, leather and metal. All have huge windows featuring cityscape and/or Biscayne Bay views - even, in most cases, from the marble bathrooms - and are adorned with mega-count linens, flat-screen TVs, Bose sound-systems and the latest business amenities. Even though the Conrad is a really a Hilton in luxury boutique attire, it's all been carried out without a corporate feel.

Style 9, Atmosphere 8, Location 6

Delano Hotel *(bottom)*
1685 Collins Avenue (17th St),
South Beach
Tel: 305 672 2000
www.delano-hotel.com
Rates: $345–1,250

Take that stereotypical representation of heaven, the far-off bright light with billowy white curtains, and then turn it 295-degrees to incorporate elements that touch on Alice in Wonderland and Liberace. That's the Delano for you. Since its opening in 1995, as Miami's reputation was becoming classier, the spot has appeared in more brochures than any other hotel on the Beach and is firmly established as a Miami landmark. The buzz in the cocktail lounges and beauty salons of South Beach, however, is that the Delano may no longer be the height of fashion. Rumour has it that it has been supplanted by a new wave of accommodation that is not so self-consciously stylish. The Delano has become the victim of its own success; indeed, it has become a bit too popular. If it didn't have such a breathtaking lobby, if Ian Schrager (co-founder of New York's Studio 54) didn't have the reputation that he does today for making such inspired hotels, and if the pool didn't have underwater music, then there would be no tourists walking around the premises taking photos. But that's Miami. On arrival, guests are escorted through the famous lobby and up to one of the 208 crisp white rooms. After arrival, head to the Aqua Spa for a massage, have a drink at the lobby's Rose Bar, check out the poolside bungalows and stick your head in the water to hear Beethoven's Third Symphony.

Style 8, Atmosphere 7, Location 9

Eden Roc *(right)*
4525 Collins Avenue, Mid-Beach
Tel: 305 531 0000
www.edenrocmiami.com
Rates: $320–950

As one of the Beach's elders, the Eden Roc deserves a measure of respect. It

made a celebrity-sparkled name for itself in the 1950s (bold names included Elizabeth Taylor, Humphrey Bogart and Harry Belafonte) and, designed by Morris Lapidus, boasts a cool architectural pedigree. In its heyday the hotel irked its neighboring competition so much that the 'bleau's owner built up a structure on his property specifically (it's said) to cast a shadow over the Eden Roc's pool in high season's peak daylight hours. (Shortly thereafter the Eden Roc unveiled a second swimming pool on the other side of the property.) Back to modern times: The hotel has recently undergone an upgrade (topping $220 million) with the addition of a luxe 22,000 sq ft spa and surf-facing fitness center (open day and night), and a new 21-floor Ocean Tower that brings the room count up to 631. There are perks installed to appeal to the gadget geeks (HDTV in the rooms, WiFi available on the beach), but they pale compared to the outdoor scene with a pod of infinity pools and yachts available for rent across the street.

Style 8, Atmosphere 8, Location 7

Epic Hotel *(top)*
270 Biscayne Boulevard Way (Brickell), Downtown
Tel: 305 424 5226,
www.epichotel.com
Rates: $240–740

With its sleek, 54-floor cylinder, this newcomer truly deserves its epithet. Surprisingly though, the Epic manages to feel intimate, with a mission that's devoted to 'reflect the values, style and attitude of everyday heroes'.

That's undoubtedly due to its parent, Kimpton Hotels, the San Francisco-based lodging corporation that imbues all its unique properties with fashionable grace. The Epic boats 411 rooms and suites, grounded in warm brown and pumpkin tones, and each features private balconies and floor-to-ceiling window walls. They are bedecked in customary Kimpton manner, with WiFi, 37-inch flat-screen TVs that swivel, Acqua di Parma bath accessories and fine Italian linens. In fact, the glass extends into the bathroom, so exhibitionists can have a field day primping and such in full view of employees in neighbouring office towers. The Asian restaurant Zuma (at street level in the same building, but unrelated to Epic) has produced a fair amount of buzz, bringing a young, fresh-thinking crowd to a somewhat tricky location.

Style 8, Atmosphere 8, Location 7

Fontainebleau *(bottom)*
4441 Collins Avenue, Mid-Beach
Tel: 877 854 2033
www.fontainebleau.com
Rates: $369–1,200

She's in her fifties, and, understandably, much bigger than she was when she first debuted. But, after her multi-year $1-billion touch-up, the Fontainebleau is back and ready for her close up. She's had a taste of glamour before, co-starring with James Bond in Goldfinger, as well as playing the perfect hostess to the Beatles, Judy Garland, Frank Sinatra and Sammy Davis Jr. in the 1950s and 1960s when Miami Beach was the US equivalent of Europe's Côte d'Azur. Emerging

sleep...

from an unfashionable decade or two, the moneyed are again clamouring to be pampered inside one of her gleaming 1,500 rooms, scattered among two buildings and two towers. The cool linens, flat-screen TVs, high-tech sound systems and iMacs in each room create a cocoon experience for agoraphobics – a difficult achievement for a property the size of the Fontainebleau. The more extroverted can flit around the 11 restaurants and clubs, recharge in the 40,000-square-foot spa, or sizzle in a cabana next to one of six jewel-like pools, or the 22 acres of adjacent beach-front. The Fontainebleau caters for all.

Style 8, Atmosphere 9, Location 7

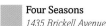

Four Seasons *(top)*
1435 Brickell Avenue
(SE 14th), Downtown
Tel: 305 358 3535
www.fourseasons.com/miami
Rates: $255–2, 550

With 70 floors, the Four Seasons Hotel and Towers building is the tallest on the Miami skyline and is visible from South Beach. Many of the Four Seasons' guests are on business, but at weekends a good proportion book in on vacation. Like the Ritz-Carlton, guests have a fair idea of what to expect – except for the art. This Four Seasons has a giant Botero sculpture in the lobby and a rotating selection of pieces (much of it by Latin American artists) strewn throughout the hotel, with every room decorated differently. The rooms all include king-size beds, as is customary, along with a soaking tub and down pillows and coverlets, and also feature

padded windowsills from which guests can look over Biscayne Bay and beyond. The 221 rooms include 39 suites, and the pool area occupies two acres in which the guests can recline and sip their drinks. The resident contemporary seafood restaurant Acqua is well rated, and the colourful 14Thirty-Five lounge can be surprisingly lively. But the biggest plus point for this hotel is the Bahia Bar. This poolside space lures in the fashionable crowd and gives a predominately business-like atmosphere a tropical kick up the ass.

Style 8, Atmosphere 7, Location 6

Gansevoort *(bottom)*
Miami Beach
2377 Collins Avenue (Espanola Way), South Beach
Tel: 305 604 1000
www.gansevoortmiamibeach.com
Rates: $250–685

This is the place where you can put your finger on the pulse of NYC amid the techno thump of South Florida. The Gansevoort Miami Beach Hotel, Spa and Residences is the sister property to the other Gansevoort that helped transform Manhattan's Meatpacking District from grit to glamour. This one has already served as the setting for a serial reality show and the entry space – a pink, yellow and white nightmare with oversized chairs and a fish-tank wall – is certainly camera-ready. You could loiter comfortably in the room (if you really wanted to) on feather beds covered in Egyptian cotton, peering at the 40-inch HDTV or steaming under the dual-head shower. But there are so many distrac-

tions, such as the not-insignificant 55,000-square-foot private beach club and the breathtaking rooftop pool and bar. The Gansevoort clan has thoughtfully imported some other familiar New York names (Phillipe Chow) to show camaraderie, but Miami native Louis, the nightspot on ground level, is reeling the masses in just fine, thank you.

Style 8/9, Atmosphere 9, Location 8

The Hotel *(left)*
801 Collins Avenue (8th St),
South Beach
Tel: 305 531 2222
www.thehotelofsouthbeach.com
Rates: $165–445

Clad in ever Miami-appropriate white-on-white, the building that now hosts the Hotel was built in 1939 by L. Murray Dixon, who designed many of the structures in the area. As it lies in the heart of the Art Deco district, no changes are allowed to the hotel's façade, but clothing designer Todd Oldham was granted open license to the inside. His understated tropical feel was unveiled at the Hotel's ribbon-cutting in 2000, and he was also charged with updating the entire building (including the noteworthy Wish restaurant and bar) on its anniversary in 2010, but the original 1939 terrazzo flooring remains. At one time this was the Tiffany Hotel, and although it lost the right to use the name, it has retained the label 'Tiffany Spire' and its adjacent bar. The octagonal pool with another pocket bar attached is the most stylish rooftop pool in Miami, with clear views of the Atlantic and the Miami skyline.

Style 8, Atmosphere 9, Location 9

Mandarin Oriental *(bottom)*
500 Brickell Key Drive, Downtown
Tel: 305 913 8288
www.mandarinoriental.com
Rates: $290–1,040

Built on Brickell Key for no less than $100 million – and renovated for its tenth anniversary in 2010 – the Mandarin Oriental is a luxurious 44-acre island overlooking Miami's financial district. Not just a hotel, it's a destination unto itself; the Oasis Beach Club and its brilliant egg-shaped bed of white sand and huge cabanas and the 17-room, 15,000-square-foot window-walled spa (where you can practise yoga, Tai Chi or Pilates) serve as significant draws. All 295 guestrooms include balconies overlooking either Biscayne Bay or the city and feature Asian-inspired lamps and artworks as well as sparkling Spanish marble bathrooms. Although the calming tone strikes you when you first stroll through the hotel into a lobby bathed in an orange glow, all is not quite as reserved as it seems. Miami's hip scenesters are drawn downstairs to the Azul restaurant, Café Sambal and M-Bar with its many martinis, so guests could happily stay at the hotel for a debauched night out without ever leaving the island.

Style 8, Atmosphere 9, Location 6

The Mercury *(right)*
South Beach
100 Collins Avenue (1st St), South Beach
Tel: 305 398 3000
www.themercurysouthbeach.com
Rates: $120–200

The unassuming Mercury is not pretentious. Its lobby is attractive but sparse, there's no humming nightclub connection, and you can't peruse the pillow menu on check-in because there isn't one. The pool is unadorned and solemn, and therefore does not aspire to be the next glitterati destination. Indeed, the Mercury is an endangered species on the southern end of South Beach. In the positive column, it's centrally located for some excellent dining (Shoji Sushi, Prime One Twelve) and is within close proximity to a fine neighbourhood bar (The Room). The management also dole out weekday passes to nearby Nikki Beach for public yet intimate lounging and snacking on private sand. In addition, all the rooms are suites, so you could conceivably stock up on groceries, take advantage of the plates and utensils in the kitchen – some have stoves – and spend all your money on alcohol.

Style 7, Atmosphere 7, Location 7

....

The National *(top)*
1677 Collins Avenue (17th St),
South Beach
Tel: 305 532 2311
www.nationalhotel.com
Rates: $270–630

To get to the heart of the National, you've got to dig a little deeper than at other upper beach hotels. It doesn't provoke with ostentatious quirkiness like the Delano, nor does it have an international reputation to fall back on like the Ritz-Carlton. And its lobby doesn't do it any favours – although the original balcony walk is an interesting touch. But the National is among the top choices

in terms of location, value and service. For instance, the stunning 205-foot pool stretches into eternity and is certainly among the most beautiful in the city, flanked by cabanas in broad brown and white striped canvas. Another attraction is the Tamara de Lempicka mosaic that casts its gaze on you as you dine in her namesake Mediterranean-fusion restaurant. The National also possesses a crack concierge team, which can put together an evening of dining and drinking, or an afternoon of scuba diving, sailing, or golf with ease (there's also a menu of a dozen or so local excursions to choose from). Rooms and suites are currently being refreshed, and the entire hotel will be sparklingly new by 2013.

Style 9, Atmosphere 8, Location 9

....

Hotel Ocean *(bottom)*
1230 Ocean Drive (12th St),
South Beach
Tel: 305 672 2579
www.hotelocean.com
Rates: $140–600

If, suddenly, you find a replica Italian piazza in the middle of Miami Beach central, you've found the discreetly marked Hotel Ocean. This unassuming inn on the Ocean Drive scene is especially notable for its awesome beach views and for its relatively affordable rack rates. Rooms are spacious and airy, with sleek furniture, dark wood or Cuban tile floors, and Italian marble bathrooms. There's not much room for snooty Miami attitude here (helped by the fact that there's no real lobby in which to be seen), and the dining option is more fun and functional than hip. It's best, then, for travellers who spend their daytime hours on the sand and their evenings under the pulsing strobes of upper-Collins nightspots.

Style 8, Atmosphere 7, Location 8

The Pelican *(top)*
826 Ocean Drive (8th St),
South Beach
Tel: 305 673 3373
www.pelicanhotel.com
Rates: $190–400

Finally, a spot where the aesthetic isn't repressed by cream and tan! This boutique hotel is backed by some serious design credibility, since it was bought and developed by the owners of Diesel. But the 27 rooms, designed by Sweden's Magnus Ehrlad, take great pains to keep your Miami experience cheeky; every door gives way to a frisky theme with a snappy name, from 'A Fortune in Aluminium' to 'Executive Zebra'. Love red? Try the popular 'Best Whorehouse'. Amenities include C.O. Bigelow bath products, audio docks and plasma/LCD TVs, and the Pelican Café fronting on Ocean Drive has its attractions as well (and also provides room service). Still unconvinced? You can make like a high-flyer by reserving the $2,500-a-night penthouse, which has three bedrooms and looks like a porn-star's palace, complete with a circular tropical fish tank embedded in a $20,000 wall of copper.

Style 9, Atmosphere 8, Location 8

The Raleigh *(bottom)*
1775 Collins Avenue (18th St),
South Beach
Tel: 305 534 6300
www.raleighhotel.com
Rates: $225–870

It's hardly advertised, but always talked about, with an entrance on a circular driveway secluded behind palm trees and hedges like a chic Palm Springs rehab centre. The Raleigh is a time-out from the hyper-competitive, all-pleasure-all-the-time Miami many have grown to love. No flurry of activity exists in the lobby, just the classic, quite capable Martini bar and a tiny café, both of which, with only limited touch-ups, date from the 1940s. The gorgeous scalloped shield of a pool – also installed in that era – feels dated in the best possible way and promotes hours of indolence. A new attraction, The Royal, a dining spot helmed by John DeLucie of New York's Waverly Inn, has also just opened. But the Raleigh is all about enjoying yourself without feeling like an item on display, as staffers in polos and white shorts cater for your every need. The rooms are spacious but are stylistically stuck back in the 1940s. Nonetheless, they are equipped with all mod-cons and have walk-in showers big enough for a small cheerleading team. You can rent a bicycle for short excursions, but if you feel the need to motor back into the twenty-first century a Vespa or Ducati can be secured for $70 a day.

Style 9, Atmosphere 9, Location 9

Ritz-Carlton *(top)*
1 Lincoln Road (Collins Ave),
South Beach
Tel: 786 276 4000
www.ritzcarlton.com
Rates: $300–1,350

Although the bones of the hotel were established at around the same time as South Beach's other Art Deco cake houses (designed in 1953 by Morris Lapidus), they're not the same bones found elsewhere on the strip. Located at the intersection of Lincoln and Collins, the Ritz-Carlton has the choicest location. The soaring and spacious twin-levelled lobby reflects the size of the guest rooms at 450-square-metres a time. Formerly the DiLido, the Ritz-Carlton – the only major hotel name in the area – was opened in 2003 after a smart $200-million refurbishment. The hotel's calling card is, of course, top-flight service; its only likely competition in North South Beach is the Fontainebleau. The property also does a brisk business with its destination spa, and the repeat guests take full advantage of the concierge team and personal shoppers. But apart from the long sandy beach full of half-naked people on the hotel's doorstep, this Ritz-Carlton does feel a lot like any other Ritz-Carlton. It's big, it's luxurious and you know exactly what you're going to get – not always a bad thing.

Style 7, Atmosphere 8, Location 9

Sagamore *(bottom)*
1671 Collins Avenue (Lincoln),
South Beach
Tel: 305 535 8088

www.sagamorehotel.com
Rates: $375–830

This is the one place where literary and artistic notables have more valuable currency than today's empty celebrities (we're talking about you, Paris). The owners, Cricket Taplin along with her husband, have been snapping up contemporary artworks since the late 1980s and have bedecked the Sagamore's public areas with their collection. Visually arresting at almost every turn, you can see why this place is dubbed 'the art hotel'. Every aspect could be an exhibition. Take, for instance, the Stairwell Project, where six artists produced six interlocking murals in a six-floor flight, or the hotel's lobby where the installations are regularly rotated, or the gallery and art video lounge. Inscriptions adorn the hallways with motivating quotes from notables such as Diego Rivers, Emerson and Delacroix. The 93 rooms – all suites of varying sizes – are soothing with pops of colour and graphic patterns sporadically placed, but they cannot compete with the myriad visions outside your door. They all incorporate whirlpool tubs with Aveda bath products, however, and have kitchenettes, plus the 24-hour room service is a great perk. The hotel also provides a pool and a spa with an outdoor terrace. So, the Sagamore is rare bird indeed; a resort space where the body is relaxed, the artistic soul is inspired and the brain is continually stimulated.

Style 9, Atmosphere 9, Location 9

St. Augustine *(left)*
347 Washington Avenue (4th St),
South Beach
Tel: 305 532 0570
www.hotelstaugustine.com
Rates: $100–250

Another find on the sleepy end of Washington Avenue, the Hotel St. Augustine has the appearance and feel of a spa without any of the actual facilities. Well, that's not entirely true, since guests can receive a multi-jet shower massage and spend time in a private steam cabin, after which they can don a fluffy robe, practise some aromatherapy and slowly sip a cocktail. All without leaving the comfort of one's room, or 'loft', as they're dubbed here. Their large maple platform beds look as if they are floating in the rooms, but because of their low placement they're inviting rather than imposing. Indeed, the Hotel St. Augustine delivers a relaxing experience instead of acting as a transit point for late-night hedonistic activities. For this, it has gained some fanatical respect, and a fan club seduced by rack rates that even those of slender means can embrace.

Style 7, Atmosphere 7, Location 7

The Savoy *(right)*
425 Ocean Drive (4th St),
South Beach
Tel: 305 532 0200
www.savoymiami.com
Rates: $190–440

The Savoy, living quietly in a largely residential area, is a sophisticated, low-key alternative for those visitors who don't live for the spotlight, even if the hotel does regularly host fashion trunk shows and weddings. The tasteful one- and two-bedroom suites (starting at 475-square-foot) allow guests to breathe, which means they won't have to traverse tiny strips of flooring to make their way around the bed. There's a competent but dull restaurant, the Terrace, which provides nourishment from dawn 'til dusk. But the Savoy's gifts are mostly water-related. As the only Ocean Drive lodging that sits directly on the beach, the Savoy commands private beach access; further, the hotel can confidently lay claim to one of the largest pool-environs south of 5th Street, if not the largest on Ocean Drive. As a bonus, the elevated sundeck lords over both the pools and the beach – why choose one when you can have both?

Style 7, Atmosphere 8, Location 7

The Setai *(bottom)*
2001 Collins Avenue (20th St),
South Beach
Tel: 305 520 6000
www.setai.com
Rates: $440–1,500

On South Beach it is easy to get distracted with talk about who is doing what where. For a moment let's forget about who bought the 6,000-square-foot Setai penthouse with a rooftop infinity pool. Let's forget which African American rock star has a recording studio on the seventh floor. Let's forget which American cyclist who won the Tour de France seven times occasionally appears here. Rather, let's focus

on the black granite bathrooms with rainfall showers and oversized bathtubs in the apartments, the Dux beds, the views of the neighbouring hotels and the Miami shoreline from high up on the Setai's tinted glass rimmed balconies. Or the Setai's luxurious spa, three pools, and the 90-foot outdoor bar. This shiny 38-floor apartment building is even more stylish than the Mandarin Oriental, more 'exclusive' than the neighbouring Shore Club, and has more efficient staff than any other hotel in Miami. Apart from the average $1,000-a-night price tag here, it's hard to pick a weakness in the Setai's armour.

Style 9, Atmosphere 10, Location 8

The Shore Club *(top)*
1901 Collins Avenue (2oth St),
South Beach
Tel: 305 695 3277 www.shoreclub.com
Rates: $345–2,200

While most reports will tell you that the Shore Club is the hottest hotel on the beach, approach Ian Schrager's Miami masterpiece with some caution. Yes, the Shore Club does have two top-class restaurants in Nobu and Ago; yes, the resident Sky Bar attracts a large number of luscious party animals; and yes, the pool areas (one Olympic-sized and the other smaller but more exclusive) are flanked with idyllic den areas. There is also an ocean-side bungalow designed for Lenny Kravitz, with its own gated pool. The staff look good in their white outfits, and the 6,000-square-foot, three-floor penthouse is sublime. But with 322 rooms

and 70 suites (designed by British architect David Chipperfield), and an additional mass of outsiders looking to eat at the restaurants and party at the Sky Bar (which produces an unending loud pump of up-to-the-minute beats), understand that the Shore Club is not a hotel from which guests leave as refreshed as they would like to. A relaxing weekend away the Shore Club is not.

Style 8, Atmosphere 9, Location 9

The Standard *(bottom)*
40 Island Avenue (Farrey),
Miami Beach
Tel: 305 673 1717
www.standardhotels.com/miami
Rates: $220–600

André Balazs kitsch cult classic comes to Miami in the form of a spa hotel, although die-hard fans of the LA outposts might be a little disappointed by the lack of retro furniture and aspiring actor staff. There's not even any significant signage, as the former Lido Beach Club is protected by historic preservation laws. This Miami Standard promises to be the epitome of holistic well-being, focusing on re-energising exhausted hedonists coming to Miami to recharge. Some spa services are available at the pool, and even the lunch and dinner menus hew closer to wholesome than decadent - it still tastes great, but you won't feel like a lazy bloated hippo the next day. Rooms, laid out lodge-style, are simple affairs dressed in white, the better to locate your pure inner self (those set off by scrims and facing the outer gardens on the first level have bathtubs situated

outside the front door, for that enervating evening soak). Situated on Belle Isle, landscaped and almost entirely residential, the Standard is well away from the frenetic activity of SoBe. The hotel's private docks and spectacular views provide tranquillity, but if you're looking for a hint of sin, a cocktail at the outdoor Fire Pit is as good as you'll get here.

Style 7, Atmosphere 6, Location 7

. . . .

The Townhouse *(top)*
150 20th Street (Collins Ave),
South Beach
Tel: 305 534 3800
www.townhousehotel.com
Rates: $115–395

The Townhouse's strengths revolve around its relaxed atmosphere, its stark, mostly white and grey minimalist décor, and its roof terrace that makes all others in Miami look shoddy. Nowhere else in Miami can guests sit on red wooden swings on the building's porch, and nowhere else does the South Beach experience feature a staff that comes equipped with an easy smile and a willingness to do more than stand and pose (well, there must be a couple somewhere). The building sits amidst some of Miami Beach's grand dames, but it doesn't have to shout to be noticed; it's thrilled to attract mere mortals who don't need to spend a $1,000 a night in order to taste the best South Beach has to offer. The Bond Street Lounge is the hotel's bar (and health-conscious sushi restaurant), but it's situated in the basement. So the roof terrace is the place

to take in the evening sunset with a caipirinha. The Townhouse, not interested in blindly following others, does not come equipped with a pool, but in a pinch, guests can take advantage of the fact that some properties welcome visitors to their pools as long as they order plenty of drinks and look good while doing so. Otherwise, bring the red-and-white sectioned inflatable ball that decorates your bed to the beach, just 50 yards away.

Style 7, Atmosphere 7, Location 8

. . . .

The Viceroy *(bottom)*
485 Brickell Avenue (SE 5th St),
Downtown
Tel: 305 503 4400
www.viceroymiami.com
Rates: $175–600

Look for the huge primitive faces of metallic moai on Brickell Avenue – they prop up the corner of the building that houses the Viceroy. Like them, the smallish, hip, futuristic lobby pops nicely, but it doesn't quite match the vibe of the rest of the hotel. Kelly Wearstler coordinated the interiors to impart a chilly, rich effect, and the layout is somewhat choppy. Vaguely Eastern patterns and furnishings temper the lushness of the décor in the common spaces and in the 168 rooms. But perhaps the crowning jewel of the Viceroy is the 15th floor, the site of two acres of 'outdoor living room' and a terrace showcasing what is claimed to be the longest infinity-edge pool in Florida (sorry, Biltmore). The welcome smacks of Alice in Wonderland, with a forest interspersed with water features, a mosaic fireplace 12-foot high and thigh-high chess pieces in blue and silver (the better to play a truly mind-bending game). There are bikes and scooters at the ready if you're up for some non-aquatic activity, but you may just keep the 'errand runners' busy and settle into your new, albeit temporary, Miami life.

Style 8, Atmosphere 9, Location 7

The Victor *(top)*
1144 Ocean Drive (12th St),
South Beach
Tel: 305 428 1234
www.hotelvictorsouthbeach.com
Rates: $300–980

In these times of climbing unemployment, the Victor has created an entirely new job title. The hotel's 'vibe manager' is charged with ensuring that the sounds and scents of the property are hip enough and inspire the moods of the guests (perhaps to drink and run up room service and spa treatment tabs?). That's probably all the outrageousness that's left from its 2005 opening, which presented a P. Diddy-hosted party, motorcycles driving through rings of fire, and a gaggle of scared (real) penguins, which created a tempest brewed by PETA (not bad for an undercover Hyatt). Without the drama, these days you can be quite comfortable in Victor's king beds and marble baths, and eat outdoors at Bice within earshot of the most aggressive restaurant hawkers on the Drive. The Victor has adopted a jellyfish theme, and there is a fascinating aquarium in the lobby, as well as images of jellyfish projected onto the hotel bar's giant screen – but this time, there's no need to call the authorities.

Style 7/8, Atmosphere 8, Location 8

The Villa *(bottom)*
by Barton G.
1116 Ocean Drive (11th St),
South Beach
Tel: 305 576 8003
www.thevillabybartong.com
Rates: $795–2,250

The main thing you need to know about this place is the V. The Villa is mostly informed by Gianni Versace, who spent five years recreating Italian architectural decadence in this spot, and who lived here the last two years of his life. That said, a stay at the hotel - or an evening in the pebble-walled dining room - is a parti-colored fever dream for anyone with designs on the jet-setting life. The kaleidoscopic Thousand Mosaic Pool is stunning (Madonna's guest bedroom overlooked it from the second floor), and each of the 10 suites – from the Aviary to the Venus – is museum-worthy. The gentleman name-checked in the property's title is Barton G. Weiss, a Miami restaurateur and world-class caterer with a decades-long history of excellence, who was tapped by the Villa's current owner to oversee operations. The only drawbacks are the imposing gate and security guard at the front (to discourage tourists) and the refined air, which will stifle any thought of ribald humour or high-spirited hijinks.

Style 9, Atmosphere 10, Location 8

Whitelaw Hotel *(above)*
808 Collins Avenue (8th St),
South Beach
Tel: 305 398 7000
www.whitelawhotelsouthbeach.com
Rates: $79–220

The 800 block of Collins is perhaps the geographic centre of (south) South Beach, with the most important clubs and dining spots only a short alcohol-fuelled stroll away. That, and the fact that the rich-feeling fashionable Whitelaw doesn't try to siphon its guests' bank accounts through its rack rates, only solidifies its worthiness. Rooms are white or flamingo pink (better than it sounds), with 42-inch flatscreens, WiFi and mini-fridges as extras (plus a free airport shuttle). Only one drawback comes as part of the package; there's no pool, only a turfed rooftop sundeck. But it's figuratively and literally cooler in the lobby, which also functions as a bar, Jiminy Cricket café (for light Italian snacks), and as a platform for special events (the Thursday Buzz, the soon-to-debut Sunday samba lessons). Sip a mid-afternoon cappuccino on the circular white leather anti-banquette, chomp on a *tramezzini*, and pity the plight of other budget-conscious travellers who don't have your keen eye, good fortune or sense of style.

Style 8, Atmosphere 8, Location 9

An Interview With Barton G.

Name: Barton G. Weiss

Are you a hedonist? I'm all about stimulating the senses in positive ways

What marks you out from the culinary crowd? I've married gastronomy with artful presentation for the last decade in my now-three restaurants, and have done the same with the culinary arts division of my company. To me, it's not just about taste, but smell, look, touch. A memorable meal should stimulate all the senses.

What defines your venues? Each of my venues is different. The Villa By Barton G. inside the former Versace Mansion is opulent, cosseted, an extension of the legacy started by designer Gianni Versace. Barton G. The Restaurant is sexy and sensual and about getting in touch with your inner child. Prelude By Barton G. marries food and performance. Each is a very different concept, but there is a Barton G. synergy that flows through them all.

What do you love about Miami? It's paradise. The sun, the sand, the architecture, the culture, the people. It really is a magical place.

In Miami, what is your favourite…
Hotel? The Villa By Barton G. I'm not just the proprietor. I check in several weekends a month. It's my getaway at home. I have a Villa Indulgence massage (eight hands, 80 minutes, always leaves me relaxed) and a leisurely dinner in The Dining Room. And try to get in some relaxation time by The Thousand Mosaic Pool.

Restaurant (aside from your own)? With three restaurants, I'm not left with much time to visit other restaurants. But the city has terrific chefs — James Beard Award winners Michelle Bernstein Michael Schwartz among them — and Miami has really come into its own as a culinary destination. When I opened my first restaurant, Barton G. The Restaurant nearly 10 years ago, the restaurant scene was very very different than it is today. Throughout Miami Beach and Miami, it's become much more textured and rich. As a restaurateur, it's kept it interesting.

Cultural sight? The new New World Symphony building by Frank Gehry. It's beyond stunning in the way it marries form with function.

Secret spot? I own a farm in Southwest Dade County where I raise organic fruits and vegetables and exotic animals including giraffes, chimps, orangutans, macaws. It's my own slice of heaven. When I'm at the farm, I feel like I'm on vacation. It allows me to be in touch with nature and the earth. It's really a very, very special place.

eat...

Miami's never been known as a foodie destination, and in most cases, rightly so. But that's not to say that it's impossible to find excellent, inspired dishes in this original city of sin. On the contrary – and regularly in the establishments associated with hotels – with a little careful consideration, fine dining is the perfect closer to a day spent roasting yourself on the white-flour beaches.

Like most things Miami, your fellow diners are probably concentrating more on how you look and the (frequently) spartan, stylish surroundings than on the quality of the plates before them. Food critics will try to convince you otherwise, but the undeniable truth is that in South Beach, people pay for the company and the location rather than what they're chomping on. Many menus offer the most elaborate fusions of flavours and styles known to man, but very often use overdressed vocabulary to disguise something far more simple (in many cases, though, the result can look ready for a food-porn close-up). Indeed, eating out here can be rather like driving a Ferrari with a Kia engine – try to see through the frills and work out what is really on offer.

As for what ends up on your plate, it's likely to follow certain conventions. Seafood is on offer almost everywhere, which is hardly surprising given the city's location, and its quality is second to none in the US. Legendary eatery Joe's Stone Crab prides itself on just one thing, and sushi hot-spots Nobu and Sushi Samba Dromo (where your sashimi arrives in an atmosphere of revelry) remain popular. With its eclectic mix of cultures, Miami has a wonderfully diverse selection of South American and Latin restaurants, from high-end establishments to those that are earthier but equally as good, serving fare from countries such as Cuba, Peru (sometimes mixed with other national cuisines), Argentina, Brazil and the Caribbean (D. Rodriguez Cuba and Versailles represent either end of the formal/casual spectrum). You can also find steakhouses serving big, bold hunks of red meat as well, though these aren't considered to be the top of the dining food chain in Miami (Smith & Wollensky is a traditional favourite, and the Meat Market is a new contender). Elsewhere on Miami's international food front, Italian food never goes out of style (Escopazzo is a particular highlight).

The majority of restaurants mentioned here lie somewhere south of 12th Street on South Beach, but that's just because SoBe is generally where you'll want to be.

Zuma

If you're really serious about your food you might be better off looking at other options where the atmosphere is slightly more formal but the food is generally superior. For instance, if you head Downtown, check out Azul in the Mandarin Oriental, with its fantastic views of the city. Alternatively, if you're intent on sampling Florida's best cooking, make the 15-minute drive from South Beach to Coral Gables. Here the chefs and restaurants take themselves very seriously, but there's usually no need to leave your open-collared shirts and tight jeans at home (though it wouldn't kill you to slip on a blazer).

Something needs to be said about service, which is severely lacking in Miami, especially when compared to other American cities like New York, San Francisco or Chicago. More often than not, your waiter seems unconcerned that his poor demeanour and/or performance will result in a miniscule tip. One final note; don't be alarmed, but the cost of fine dining in the 3-0-5 is among the highest in the country. The price of appetisers frequently lands north of $10, and it's not uncommon for mains to stretch into the mid-$30s. But no one comes to Miami to scrimp (or indeed, save).

The restaurants listed here are all rated for food, service and atmosphere and the price given is for two courses for one, with half a bottle of wine.

The Villa by Barton G.

the best restaurants...

Our favourites:
Azul
Casa Tua
La Cofradia
The Forge
Mercadito
Nobu
Ola
The River
The Villa by Barton G
Wish

For Food:
Azul
Casa Tua
The Forge
The Villa by Barton G
Wish

For Service:
Azul
La Cofradia
The River
The Villa by Barton G
Wish

For Atmosphere:
Casa Tua
The Forge
Nobu
Sushi Samba Dromo
The Villa by Barton G

Abokado *(left)*
900 South Miami Avenue
(SE 9th St), Downtown
Tel: 305 347 3700
www.abokadosushi.com
Open: noon–3pm, 5.30–11pm (midnight
Fri/Sat, 10pm Sun). Closed Sun lunch.
$58   ***Sushi/Seafood***

Folks who work in the banks and real estate offices in the Downtown corridor look forward to their weekly lunch among their peers at Abokado. This restaurant, IKEA-catalogue ready and placed in the centre of Mary Brickell Village, is that rare no-fuss, low-maintenance sushi option where there's not much concern for appearances (but don't worry, the fish and crustaceans here have been well cared for before they appear on your plate). The usual suspects are in attendance on the bill of fare, plus a few things that seem, well, a bit foreign to Asian templates (spicy tuna 'nachos'? crab mix and chorizo-stuffed calamari?). Nonetheless, the ingredients are fresh, and if given the opportunity, would walk off the plate.

Food 8, Service 7, Atmosphere 7

Azul *(right)*
Mandarin Oriental Hotel,
500 Brickell Key Drive, Downtown
Tel: 305 913 8254
www.mandarinoriental.com
Open: 7–11pm Mon–Sat
$120   ***Mediterranean Fusion***

Located in the tiny Mandarin Oriental on Brickell Key, Azul is the only restaurant in the city with both Biscayne Bay and Downtown skyline views. Said maritime and cosmopolitan vistas can be admired from the nicely breezy outdoor terrace or inside behind glorious floor-to-ceiling windows. But once the plates are set down, all eyes are on the mostly seafood-based mains, which are marvellously prepared and presented (forgive them if the menu descriptions contain too many ingredients and somewhat frou-frou titles that include phrases such as 'a study in tuna'). The open kitchen, clad in white marble, is state-of-the-art and helmed by executive chef Joel Huff. It's been cited as the city's standout hotel restaurant (Miami Herald) and also – with more than 700 well-considered selections – for its 'Best Wine Service' (Miami Magazine). Thus, Azul, oozing sophistication, is one of Miami's top reservations. For pre- or post-dinner drinks, M-Bar at the other end of the Mandarin Oriental's lobby boasts an impressive 250 varieties of Capital Martini in its armoury.

Food 8, Service 9, Atmosphere 8

Barton G *(bottom)*
1427 West Avenue (14th),
South Beach
Tel: 305 672 8881 www.bartong.com
Open: daily, 6–10.30pm
(midnight Sat/Sun)
$85   ***Modern American/Caribbean***

The unique, inventive Barton G is a bit of an enigma, in the best possible way, so it continually confounds expectations. It's named after the principal Barton G. Weiss, a globally-recognised event planner to billion-dollar corporations and high-profile celebs. This well-regarded spot – on the west side of the

peninsula, well removed from the heavily travelled Ocean Drive – combines Pan-Asian and Caribbean influenced dishes with updated takes on classic American staples (fried chicken, mac 'n' cheese) and somehow makes it work. Oh, and there's an occasional detour into molecular gastronomy (interesting appetisers, cocktails made using liquid nitrogen) and a healthy sense of humour too (swordfish served... on a sword!). Corporate executive chef Ted Mendez has been with Barton G since it opened in 2002, and the menu retains his stamp of playfulness and accessibility. The main room is elegant and well-lit, but for a lush alternative, dine in the orchid garden.

Food 8, Service 8, Atmosphere 8

Blue Door Fish   *(top)*
Delano Hotel, 1685 Collins Avenue (17th St), South Beach
Tel: 305 674 6400
www.delano-hotel.com
Open: daily, 11am–4pm, 7–11pm
$80   *Fish / Seafood*

Once upon a time, long ago in the 1990s, Madonna co-owned Blue Door at the Delano. It was almost impossible to book a table, the girls were beautiful, the men spent obscene amounts of cash and everybody was happy – until people realised the food wasn't any good. Under the brow of restaurateur Jeffrey Chodorow and executive chef Claude Troisgros, the restaurant's reputation for fine dining was restored, and further cemented with its evolution into Blue Door Fish in October 2010. Blue Door builds on the excess of the rest

of the Delano Hotel. The menu used to whisper French refinement, but the new attention paid to fruits de mer and the unexpected Brazilian accents (such as the cashews and palmitos scattered throughout the menu and the roasted lobster with caramelised banana brown butter) make for a better fit in this venue. All the feasting takes place in a space reminiscent of a weekend in a low-lit Las Vegas establishment, with white leather banquettes and mirrors and bling aplenty instead of neon. Weekend brunch is still quite popular, and this remains the time when the idea of French refinement goes out the window.

Food 8, Service 7, Atmosphere 8

Caffe Abbracci   *(bottom)*
318 Aragon Avenue (Salzedo),
Coral Gables
Tel: 305 441 0700
www.caffeabbracci.com
Open: daily, 11.30am–3.30pm, 6pm–midnight. Closed Sat/Sun lunch.
$66   *Italian*

Even from the outside, where a few street-side tables sit before a wall of faux-wood panelling, it appears as the setting for a gangster flick assassination, wherein hugs before appetisers morph into bullets before dessert. As such, Caffe Abbracci exudes anti-Miami style; that is, dark and darker. The multi-fingered, pendulous, red-glass Chihuly fixture in the main dining room is a nice touch, as is the huge stained-glass tray ceiling in the handsome bar area, but they don't brighten up the place and don't succeed in their attempt at romanticism. In short, the restaurant's Goodfellas-era look could do with a style intervention. The plates are regarded by the locals as very good and dependable rather than exceptional, but the service is attentive, and the combination has enabled Caffe Abbracci to weather the cycle of Miami's ever-changing culinary fascinations and the fickleness of the city's diners. Expect Italian staples built on traditional recipes and a decent selection of fish; the black ravioli lobster is definitely worth a try.

Food 7, Service 8, Atmosphere 7

Casa Tua *(top)*
1700 James Avenue (17th St),
South Beach
Tel: 305 673 1010
www.casatualifestyle.com
Open: daily, 7–11pm (midnight Sat/Sun)
$120 **Italian**

The proprietors of this restaurant want to make you feel truly welcome, almost as if you were dining well at 'the home of a good friend'. Casa Tua is a 1925 two-tiered Mediterranean Revivalist villa, nestled away behind hedges and an iron gate (for that air of exclusivity). In addition to the upper floor that serves as a five-room boutique hotel, the place offers upscale Italian food in a friendly, relaxed atmosphere that is often hard to find in Miami. You are greeted by the owner, an ex-polo patron from a wealthy family, and his stunning hostesses. They happily welcome the well-healed clientele, whom they seat at a smart communal dining table or at one of the few tables in a garden of herbs and flowers that produces blooms for every table. Casa Tua will smash your Miami budget to pieces,

but most people say it is worth it. It has a devoted following, and there's a private clubroom upstairs for 'members' who pay $4,000 a year for the privilege, but there's no need; the more intimate bar off the restaurant should suit you fine.

Food 9, Service 8, Atmosphere 9

China Grill *(bottom)*
404 Washington Avenue (4th St),
South Beach
Tel: 305 534 2211
www.chinagrillmgt.com
Open: daily, noon–midnight
(1am Fri/Sat, 10pm Sun)
$64 **International Fusion**

This southern spin-off of Manhattan's critically acclaimed China Grill is one of South Florida's most popular dining meccas, even after more than a decade. From a distance its illuminated multicoloured tower looks more like a car park, casino and strip club than a restaurant. In fact, quite a few years ago the building was featured prominently in the exterior shots for an adult movie dealing with a Russian vs. Columbian mafia theme. The grill's menu is similarly international – they call it 'world cuisine', and that's entirely accurate for a fusion of Italian, Japanese, French, Chinese, Thai and American ingredients. Signature dishes include lobster pancakes stir-fried with red chilli, coconut milk and scallions, and duck two ways. Portions are very generous and dishes are meant to be shared (although you can still order half portions), while the wine list is comprehensive and expensive. If you are feeling more Japanese than Chinese, the

Dragon sushi bar has been added on as a separate entity.

Food 8, Service 7, Atmosphere 7

La Cofradia *(top)*
160 Andalusia Avenue (Ponce De Leon Blvd), Coral Gables
Tel: 305 914 1300 www.lacofradia.com
Open: 11.30am–2.30pm (Tues–Fri), 6pm–10pm (11.30pm Thurs–Sat). Closed Sundays and Mondays.
$80   **Mediterranean / Peruvian**

This time it's Mediterranean and not the usual Asian fare that gets the opportunity to interact with Peruvian sensibilities. The two mesh well at La Cofradia, an establishment in Coral Gables that provides some interesting diversions. The preparations sample heavily from France and Italy, and make free use of Peruvian staples like corn, cilantro, chiles, lime, custard apple and pisco (the country's equivalent to brandy). The *chupe de camarones* (traditional shrimp soup), ceviches and seared tuna with dark cilantro sauce are quite flavourful, and even the dishes that seemingly don't fit the programme (like the short ribs marinated – poetically – for a day in Cabernet) are still winners. As far as aesthetics go, the slate floors and dark walnut accents in the dining area would normally make the space cold. However, La Cofradia, with one wall outlined by underlit blocks and an Italian-style mural of a semi-nude woman smirking down at you from the ceiling, is unquestionably one of the most sensual restaurants in all of South Florida.

Food 8, Service 9, Atmosphere 8

D. Rodriguez *(bottom)*
Cuba On Ocean
Hilton Bentley South Beach, 101 Ocean Drive (1st St), South Beach
Tel: 305 672 6624
www.drodriguezcuba.com
Open: 6–11pm (midnight Fri / Sat, 10pm Sun / Mon)
$77   **Cuban**

Newsweek magazine titled him 'one of the 100 Americans who will influence the coming millennium'; a strong endorsement for anyone's résumé, let alone a chef's. Now a legitimate South Beach celebrity (and quite the character), chef Douglas Rodriguez has several game-changing properties to his credit, including Ola (see separate entry), and this dining room, which opened at the Astor Hotel in 2009. Much more narrowly focused than Ola, this restaurant honours its Cuban roots with traditional cuisine elevated to fine dining status. The *ropa vieja* flatbread is a fine starter, and together with the more refined *enchilado* lobster or the crispy-skin pork entrée ensures you'll be quite sated by the end of the evening. Plates are presented in an airy but rich-looking room beneath framed black and white portraits and, on one side, by an enormous wine wall. After dinner, on a patio illuminated by hanging lanterns, you can dream of driving a classic sedan along Havana's Malecón while smoking a cigar chosen from 20 varieties in the restaurant's humidor.

Food 8, Service 8, Atmosphere 8

eat...

Eos *(left)*

*The Viceroy, 485 Brickell
Avenue (SE 5th St), Downtown
Tel: 305 503 0373
www.viceroymiami.com
Open: 11am–3.30pm, 7–10pm
(11pm Fri/Sat). No dinner Sun.*
$52 **Modern Greek**

Executive chef Michael Psilakis, the
so-called master of modern-era (post-
2005) Greek food in the States, is the
one to credit with Eos' ethos. Don't worry if visions of *spanikopita* and roasted
lamb don't appeal, though, since the
menu doesn't read as particularly Hellenic (the only exceptions are some
regional cheeses, references to Greek
'salad' and 'paella', and a sprinkling of
olives). The periodic table *de cuisine* is
somewhat heavily skewed towards its
seafood elements, with seven sashimis
and four ceviches among the starters
and a simply grilled whole *loup de mer*
among the mains. Like the customers,
many of whom are ensconced at the hotel, the dishes are carefully put together
and thoughtfully plated, not a stray pea
tendril or errant dot of sauce in sight.
The linear-feel dining room is large but
tame, and one can easily find a corner
in which to avoid scrutiny if necessary.

Food 8, Service 8, Atmosphere 7

Escopazzo *(bottom)*

*1311 Washington Avenue (13th St),
South Beach
Tel: 305 674 9450 www.escopazzo.com
Open: 6–11pm. Closed Mondays.*
$79 **Italian**

The term 'organic Italian' sounds a bit
humdrum; Escopazzo is anything but.
Fans of chef Giancarla Bodoni's restaurant rave about the asparagus flan and
the pumpkin ravioli, but in truth, Escopazzo offers up a lot to talk about. Great
care is taken with the plates and the
menu, which includes sections devoted
to cheeses and raw foods. In 1993,
owner Pino Bodini put 10 tables at the
front of his family home and called it
Escopazzo. Back then, his mother would
shout advice from the back of the kitch-
en while she cooked tiramisu. Now, this
cosy upscale Italian restaurant feels like
the innocent little lamb of Washington
Avenue, flanked by tattoo parlours and
novelty shops. Nonetheless, it has its devoted following of regulars and the occasional movie star visitor to boot.

Food 8, Service 8, Atmosphere 7

The Forge *(right)*

*432 Arthur Godfrey Road
(Sheridan Ave), Mid-Beach
Tel: 305 538 8533 www.theforge.com
Open: daily, 6pm–midnight (1am Fri/Sat)*
$90 **Modern American**

Steeped in history, the Forge sometimes
seems as if it was the foundation on
which Miami was built. Opened as an
extension to existing ironworks in the
1930s, the restaurant was the place
where mobsters, presidents and movie
stars would dine shoulder-to-shoulder.
Redesigned by international mogul Al
Malnik in 1969 and stocked with much
of his private collection of art and antiques, it was immediately heralded as
Miami's most glamorous destination,
attracting a glittering cast of legendary

figures including Frank Sinatra and Richard Nixon. These days – after another extensive restoration in 2009 – activity at the Forge centres at the bar, which separates three adjoining dining areas. The rooms are all wood-panelled with stained-glass ceilings and windows that overlook a mix of hip SoBe scenesters, wannabe gangsters who chomp firmly on cigars, and ageing Miami upper-crusters. The food at the Forge, newly focused on a 'farm-to-table' aesthetic and centred on beef, lamb, fish and crustaceans, is excellent. But perhaps the most impressive aspect is the eight-room wine cellar of 300,000 vintages, which covers a list 50 pages long.

Food 9, Service 8, Atmosphere 9

Joe's Stone Crab *(top)*
*11 Washington Avenue
(S Pointe Dr), South Beach*
Tel: 305 673 0365
www.joesstonecrab.com
*Open: 11.30am–2pm, 5–10pm (11pm
Fri/Sat). Closed Sun/Mon lunch.*
$75 *Seafood*

If in doubt, South Beach locals will always point visitors in the direction of the world-famous Joe's Stone Crab. In 1913, Joe Weiss, the man who claimed to have discovered the edible virtues of the stone crab, opened up Joe's Stone Crab for business and created Miami Beach's monument to informal fine-dining, a place where Al Capone, J. Edgar Hoover and the Kennedys used to hang out. The seasonal stone crabs are served in a delicious mustard sauce, the recipe for which is apparently as secret as the formula for Coca–Cola.

For non-crab lovers there are other dishes, but if that's the case, why even bother, as it would be a shame to ignore this restaurant's signature dish. This is not an intimate dining location, but the atmosphere and ultra-efficient service make for a satisfying outing. It doesn't take reservations, so it's first come first served, and some will wait for hours. This is a touristy scene, but the food is too good to ignore.

Food 9, Service 9, Atmosphere 7

La Locanda *(bottom)*
*413 Washington Avenue (4th St),
South Beach*
Tel: 305 538 6277
*Open: daily, noon–midnight
(1am Sat/Sun)*
$60 *Italian*

This little bambino is owned and run by an ex-undefeated Italian boxer and an ex-Italian paratrooper, and is hands down the friendliest restaurant on South Beach. Francesco Cavalletti, who once had a promotional contract with Don King, and Massimo Fortunato, who used to jump out of aeroplanes over enemy territory, have created a charming trattoria that somehow seats 60 people. The menu is not overly adventurous, but chef Roberto Lopez and his assistant make good use of the miniscule kitchen and brick pizza oven to produce some fabulous dishes that have turned locals into loyalists. La Locanda is also moderately priced, thus the SoBe Ferrari crowd tends to turn up their noses. But for those in the know who go early to commandeer the outside tables.

Food 8, Service 8, Atmosphere 7

....

■ **Meat Market** *(top)*
915 Lincoln Road (Jefferson),
South Beach
Tel: 305 532 0088
www.meatmarketmiami.com
Open: daily, 6pm (4pm Sun)–
midnight (1am Fri/Sat)
$104 **Steak**

Obviously, this is a Meat Market (noun): 1. meeting place for single people, 2. butcher's shop. To wit: its seductive glow draws hordes of lithe and/or brawny customers in to stand and look fabulous while awaiting their reservations, gulping pisco sours. Executive chef Sean Brasel, a favourite son of Miami from his time commanding the kitchen at Touch restaurant, is on board here to oversee a veritable warehouse full of beef in a sizeable array of cuts. If you're the adventurous type – you are in Miami, after all – choose the ancho-and-coffee fillet or the buffalo tenderloin that comes with a bittersweet chocolate mole butter. In fact, a short addendum of 'rich steak butters', superfluous in expression and execution, can be applied to any dish here for anyone who finds that rich, juicy, fat-marbled steak can't be fully appreciated without some additional fat on top (they keep the likes of African pheasant, lobster or sea bass available for card-carrying red meat-phobes). Plenty of hedonists will still be at the bar when you depart, fat, happy and ready to graze among the rest of Lincoln Road's attractions.

Food 9, Service 8, Atmosphere 8

....

■ **Mercadito** *(bottom)*
3252 NE 1st Avenue
(Midtown Blvd), Downtown
Tel: 786 369 0430
www.mercaditorestaurants.com
Open: daily, 11.30am–midnight
(1am Thurs, 2am Fri/Sat)
$60 **Mexican**

This new entry on the Miami dining landscape generated buzz immediately upon opening in 2010. Mercadito originated in New York City where it's still quite popular, but an outpost of the upscale(ish) Mexican street food canteen in Miami is a no-brainer. The menu's winning guacamole section makes the case that plain avocado is passé, with intensely flavourful breeds that use pumpkin, jicama, mango or sautéed Serrano chiles as top notes. Tacos (flat, open, four to an order), *taquizas* and ceviches are well-prepared, nicely spiced and more filling than they sound. The backdrop of vibrant Latin-inflected wall decorations, more New York City arts district than dusty Juarez calle, keeps things festive, as does the gorgeous hammered copper sheeting installed behind the bar. But it's the availability and treatment of Mexican firewater that raises the stakes and transforms Mercadito from an interesting snackery into a respected dining space that's also casual and joyful. Have one of the lipsmackingly tasty tequila or mescal cocktails with your meal, or choose a designated driver and order one of the six dozen *blancos*, *reposados* and *añejos* – the three ages of tequila – represented here. Just don't hold us responsible.

Food 8, Service 9, Atmosphere 9

....

Nobu *(top)*
The Shore Club, 1901 Collins Avenue (20th St), South Beach
Tel: 305 695 3100
www.noburestaurants.com/miami
Open: daily, 7pm–11pm
$90 *Japanese/Peruvian*

The Nobu brand can now be found in more than 20 outposts in locations as far afield as Dubai and Waikiki, but its culinary legacy is in no danger of being diluted. Hidden at the back of the Shore Club hotel, the room still attracts both the hoi-polloi and persons who are very serious about the sea-sourced items on their plates. For anyone unfamiliar with the menu, selections here range from the simple and perfectly treated (Kumomoto oysters, ceviche) to the lush-tasting and elegant. The menu is quite extensive, encompassing hot and cold dishes, sushi, sashimi and 'mains' (*omakase*, tempuras, teriyakis and the like). Of course, Nobu's signature black cod with miso is still amazing; it's the dish that redefined what Japanese food could aim for. Reservations are recommended. If your concierge fails to land a table for you, the alternative is to turn up and hope there is room at the bar area, where ultra-toned bartenders look after rowdy businessmen and where cosmopolitan-drinking blondes wait to pick up someone suitably sexy.

Food 9, Service 8, Atmosphere 9

Norman's 180 *(middle)*
180 Aragon Avenue (Ponce De Leon Blvd), Coral Gables
Tel: 305 529 5180
www.normans180.com
Open: daily, 6pm–midnight
$59 *Modern American*

The original Norman's in Coral Gables was one of the most famous restaurants in the area since its chef, Norman Van Aken, put South Florida on the culinary map, so to speak, with New World cuisine, a fusion of native and island ingredients informed by a thorough knowledge of French cooking techniques. His newest entry, opened in 2010, is something of a dramatic change, with a reliance on locally-sourced ingredients and simpler techniques (hence the '180' of the name, referring both to the Aragon Avenue address and the degrees of difference from the idea of the former place). The options are generally American rib-sticking fare, though the words 'paella', 'pho', and 'escabeche' all make an appearance on the menu. Norman's 180 is still in the process of picking up additional loyalists, so its central Gables location attached to the Westin Colonnade hotel is key. The atmosphere is always friendly, and you can enjoy a casual meal and a draft at the bar if you so choose.

Food 9, Service 8, Atmosphere 8

Ola *(bottom)*
Sanctuary Hotel, 1745 James Avenue (17th St), South Beach
Tel: 305 695 9125
www.olamiami.com
Open: daily, 6–11pm (1am Sat/Sun)
$70 *Latin American*

Chef Douglas Rodriguez gained foodie props for Yuca in Coral Gables and Patria in New York City back in the 90s. Ola (which opened in

Downtown in 2003 but moved here in 2008) produces a serious mixture of Latin-American recipes that most chefs in Miami would never consider. Ceviches, however, are what Douglas is renowned for; in fact, he has written a book called *The Great Ceviche.* The menu is anchored by ten worthy choices but two, the wahoo (it's a fish) and the fire-and-ice, are standouts, creating acidic heat and soothing it simultaneously (with cucumber sorbet and pear granita, respectively). The rest of the card, like a name-dropping CEO, references a number of Caribbean and South American nations, though the carefully prepared combinations hang together nicely. Additionally, Ola offers ceviche and mojito making classes for groups, so you can export something of the chef's hand to wherever you call home.

Food 9, Service 9, Atmosphere 9

....

■ **Ortanique** *(top)*
278 Miracle Mile
(Salzedo), Coral Gables
Tel: 305 446 7710
www.cindyhutsoncuisine.com
Open: 11.30am–2.30pm (Mon– Fri),
6–10pm (11pm Thurs–Sat, 9.30pm Sun)
$65 *International / Caribbean*

She studied the great television chefs for many years and picked up tips from a friend's restaurateur father. Then self-taught chef and co-owner Cindy Hutson moved to Miami and set out on the ocean, acting as skipper on a 36-foot fishing boat and testing out her culinary ideas on the fish that were caught for the passengers and crew.

Eventually she brought her seafaring knowledge back to dry land to start a South Beach restaurant before opening Ortanique in the Coral Gables restaurant arena. Ortanique specialises in 'Cuisine of the Sun', an invented concept cobbled from South America, Asia, North America and the Caribbean. Jamaican spices and techniques figure prominently, since the country was the homeland of Hutson's first husband and the base for her first business venture, a coffee and seasoning exporting company. The restaurant's name relates to a Caribbean strain of oranges, and indeed, the curtains, doors, plates, menus, pillars and tables at the restaurant are all decorated with orange motifs. It's pretty, if a bit much, but in any case Ortanique serves some excellent signature dishes (mussels in spicy Jamaican Red-Stripe beer broth, West Indian-style bouillabaisse). Chefs in the area always recommend this restaurant and it is regularly packed, so she's doing something right.

Food 9, Service 8, Atmosphere 7

....

■ **Osteria del Teatro** *(bottom)*
1443 Washington Avenue (Espanola), South Beach
Tel: 305 538 7850
www.osteriadelteatromiami.com
Open: 6–11pm. Closed Sundays.
$60 *Italian*

While Osteria del Teatro may not be the trendiest venue in South Beach, it is certainly one of the most famous. The mouthwatering menu on offer at this award-winning Italian is so good that its tiny dining area (seating just 30) brims

with tourists and locals every night of the week, come rain or shine. Take no notice of the pink menus; instead listen to your waiter reel off a long list of ever-changing specials, all of which live up to their poetic promise. The design is a simple combination of white tablecloths and bright walls topped off with a selection of fiery modern paintings.

Food 8, Service 7, Atmosphere 7

Por Fin *(top)*
2500 Ponce de Leon Boulevard
(Andalusia Ave), Coral Gables
Tel: 305 441 0107
www.porfinrestaurant.com
Open: daily, 11.30am–10pm
(11pm Fri / Sat)
$70   **Spanish / Mediterranean**

The businessmen and shopaholics who eat at the semi-refined Por Fin seek a certain elevation from their dining experiences, and they'll find it here, with a mood that can be described as 'Barcelona by day', simultaneously a bit formal and familiar. The tables are crisply attired in white with glinting silverware amid columns and burnished wood, while the attentive servers are impeccably attired in basic black. Guests are spoiled for choice, with twenty starters and a dozen wines by the glass to open their palates before tackling the Spanish-Mediterranean menu. However, it is the quality of the food that is the key to Por Fin's popularity (the mostly reasonable prices help as well). The first item listed on the menu is particularly recommended; a classic *pa amb tomàquet* which is explosively flavoured despite its simple composition. The delicate-yet-substantial short ribs get high marks from everyone who finds

them on their table, and they're just about perfect after a day of strolling down Coral Gables' sunny avenues.

Food 8, Service 7, Atmosphere 7

Prime One Twelve *(bottom)*
112 Ocean Drive
(1st St), South Beach
Tel: 305 532 8112
www.mylesrestaurantgroup.com
Open: daily, noon–3pm, 5.30pm–
midnight (1am Fri / Sat)
$100   **Steak**

Prime One Twelve is, unapologetically, a steakhouse. If you're vegetarian, do not approach the bar (or the dining room for that matter) – apparently peanuts went out of style years ago and bacon is back in fashion. Bacon, aside this is among the most notably hip eating spots south of 5th Street, so even if you do book a table you will be sent to the exceptionally stylish but crowded bar. The main dining area is on the ground floor and handsomely masculine, the brick and dark wood softened (a bit) by the shimmer of glassware and the crisp white of the chairs and tablecloths (a couple more intimate dining rooms are situated upstairs). Although the restaurant does offer some delicate alternatives, it would be a shame not to indulge in the rather expensive yet tender steaks served here. Afterwards, a stop nearby at the Room might serve as a bridge before an evening of concerted bar-hopping elsewhere.

Food 9, Service 5, Atmosphere 8

Le Provencal *(left)*
*266 Miracle Mile
(Salzedo), Coral Gables*
Tel: 305 448 8984
www.leprovencalrestaurant.com
Open: daily, noon–10pm
$61 **French**

Le Provencal finds itself a newcomer on this block after spending 20 years a few doors away as the Gables' favourite French bistro. The methods and ingredients of southern France were imported to South Florida via chefs Terrou and Antoniotti, who spent their culinary education at restaurants in Cassis, Souillac and Cannes (with stops in London, St. Moritz and Bogota along the way). The meals at Le Provencal are expertly finished, and among the expected preparations (bouillabaisse, veal scaloppini) are a few that will surprise (such as roast duck in honey and figs or salmon in lemongrass and saffron). The restaurant is not sufficiently ballsy to gamble on a lavender colour scheme, but the cobalt blue on display is festive enough. A simplified bar menu is served from 3pm to 7pm, when *croque madame* cravings typically kick into high gear.

Food 8, Service 8, Atmosphere 7

The River Seafood *(right)*
& Oyster Bar
*650 S Miami Avenue (SW 7th St),
Downtown*
Tel: 305 530 1915
www.therivermiami.com
*Open: 11.30am–5pm (Mon–Fri), 6–
10.30pm (midnight Fri/Sat). Closed Sun.*
$67 **Seafood**

One wouldn't customarily go Downtown (especially to this part of Downtown) to find a classy fish joint. However, the River is an unusual breed that has high aspirations yet doesn't put itself on a pedestal (note the prominently displayed life-size Johnny Cash poster that the singer signed and gave to the owner). On a serious note, chef and restaurateur David Bracha has had 20 years in the briny – seven of them here – and he knows what he's doing. The place starts buzzing Friday nights pre-dinner, when local business owners and female politicos chat around the slate and mahogany bar (specialty beers on tap and an award-winning wine list are the River's liquid strong points). Customers keep coming here for the bivalves and seafood, with a variety of bracingly fresh selections that change nightly. Whole Key's yellowtail snapper main and the lobster cocktail opener are fine starting points. Though the cavernous clubs are not far, the River is best for a night when you won't be dancing later; crustaceans and bouncing bodies don't mix.

Food 8, Service 9, Atmosphere 8

Shoji Sushi *(bottom)*
*100 Collins Avenue (1st St),
South Beach*
Tel: 305 532 4245
www.mylesrestaurantgroup.com
Open: daily, noon–midnight (1am Fri/Sat)
$60 **Sushi**

Shoji Sushi practically invented sushi on South Beach, and nearing its 10th anniversary, has outlasted much of its competition. The restaurant is in a prime location steps away from the entry to the Mercury South Beach, and light

years from the tourist dining traps of Ocean Drive and their upper-level decibel count, but you can still partake in some posturing with your fellow diners staying at the Savoy or coming off Nikki Beach. Mostly, though, it's a relaxing spot to nibble on some of the best fish in town and sip from many, many flasks of cold sake. We recommend skipping the *teriyaki* and *kushiyaki* diversions and immersing yourself in sushi rolls (especially the Shoji special and the 'dynamite'). The service is tight here, and the waiters will never allow your glass to be empty. The food is also offered at an attractive price point, so expect a combination of up-and-coming fashion photographers, models who haven't hit the big time and the usual Miami Beach big-shots.

Food 8, Service 8, Atmosphere 8

Smith & Wollensky   *(left)*
1 Washington Avenue (at South Pointe Park), South Beach
Tel: 305 673 2800
www.smithandwollensky.com
Open: daily, noon–midnight (2am Fri/Sat)
$97   **Steak/Grill**

If you're in the mood for a wonderfully bright-tasting, sizeable hunk of steer, this is the best place in Miami to feast. This Floridian branch of a national name is adjacent to a grassy park at the southernmost tip of Miami Beach, thus affording a spectacular view. The vista encompasses the windows of Downtown and Miami's main shipping channel, so yachts, big vulgar speedboats and gigantic cruise ships pass by as you sip your first Manhattan. Selected from the top two per cent of those American cuts designated as 'prime', the beef is carved up by the house butchers for optimal fat-to-flavour ratio. There's a choice of fillet, rib-eye, sirloin, prime rib and porterhouse, along with some similarly high-quality (and skilfully, unfussily prepared) lamb, sea bass, lobster and shellfish. This is one of the very few restaurants on South Beach to actually overlook the water, and it's often packed, so it's definitely advisable to reserve a table outside for full effect.

Food 8, Service 7, Atmosphere 8

Spiga   *(right)*
1228 Collins Avenue (12th St), South Beach
www.spigarestaurant.com
Tel: 305 534 0079
Open: daily, 6–11pm (11.30pm Fri/Sat)
$56   **Italian**

Spiga ('wheat' in Italian) has been on South Beach for close to 15 years, which in Miami terms means the food has continued to attract customers long after the restaurant has become old news. Clean lines, white tablecloths and a wooden bar make this is very welcoming, down-to-earth Italian. It is not quite in the same league as Escopazzo or Casa Tua because the menu is not as adventurous and, Spiga is not as ambitious as its Italian counterparts. But with a constantly changing and properly priced specials board as well as its pasta, risotto and fish staples, Spiga is an underestimated dining venue. And all the cooler for it.

Food 8, Service 8, Atmosphere 7

Sugarcane   *(bottom)*
3250 NE 1st Avenue (Midtown Blvd), Downtown

Tel: 786 369 0353
www.sugarcanerawbargrill.com
Open: daily, 11.30am–midnight
(1am Thurs, 2am Fri/Sat)
$69 *International/South American*

The beamed ceilings and oversized fans inside Sugarcane bring to mind Cuba, plantations and hurricanes. That signals this eatery as something of an abrupt departure from the same team's earlier project, the bouncy upscale temple to fish and festivity that is Sushi Samba Dromo. The capable Timon Balloo, executive chef here, created a menu in several seemingly unconnected milieus – simple Japanese robataya grill, raw bar, sushi and lush-sounding tapas plates – that holds well together. The only downside is a bill steeper than you'd imagined. This restaurant, new in 2010, has been extremely well received by the public and critics alike, but outside peak weekend hours, the need for reservations is unlikely due to the size of the space. For a more romantic vibe, ask to sit in the garden, surrounded by ivy-covered trees and shrubbery under strung-up white star lanterns.

Food 9, Service 8, Atmosphere 8

Sushi Samba Dromo *(top)*
600 Lincoln Road
(Pennsylvania Ave), South Beach
Tel: 305 673 5337
www.sushisamba.com
Open: daily, noon–midnight (1am Wed/ Thur/Sun, 2am Fri/Sat)
$61 *Japanese/Brazilian/Peruvian*

No longer as daring a concept as when it was introduced in the late 90s in New York, the hybrid Japanese-Brazilian-

Peruvian offerings at Sushi Samba Dromo are still fun, even if they don't represent the height of contemporary dining. The menu, a bit of a jumble, is chopped up into no less than nine categories, including the traditional multi-course Japanese omakase meal and churrasco (the Brazilian meatfest, stripped of its usually integral 'unlimited' element). The Samba rolls are stuffed to the gills with ingredients; if that's not your thing, try some of the large plates, like the moqueca (Brazilian shrimp stew) or Peruvian duck chife. Almost as luscious-looking as the plates is the coterie of customers (consisting largely of thin young businessfolk and their arm candy, celebs, or groups of raucous twentysomethings) and staffers (often model-wannabes somehow landed in the wrong city, with the proper peevish attitude to match). Thankfully, washed in sunset colours and constructed with a great reliance on curves, the main room has been composed for everyone's maximum visibility.

Food 7, Service 7, Atmosphere 9

Talavera *(bottom)*
2299 Ponce de Leon Boulevard
(Giralda), Coral Gables
Tel: 305 444 2955 www.talaveraspot.com
Open: daily, 11.30am–10pm
(11pm Thurs–Sat)
$42 *Mexican*

Miami is usually so busy promoting the culture and cuisines of Latin America and the Caribbean that Mexico is largely left out of the picture. If you're curious as to what an expert hand can do with authentic Mexican food, seek out Talavera. Mexico City native and Johnson & Wales graduate Oscar del Rivero is an accomplished chef who toiled at Miami Beach's Blue Door, the respected-but-now-closed Talula and the Palm Hotel. Regardless of the level of spiciness, intense flavours abound. The creamy guacamole, prepared to order, is a must, and the moles, fish (with clams in *salsa verde*) and beef Don Guillermo (under a blanket of *huitlacoche*, cheese and *poblano* cream sauce) are first-rate. There are a couple dozen wines on the list, but when in Rome... order a margarita (choose from original, creative, ambitious or old-fashioned). The restaurant has a grand adobe brick-hued dining space accented with clean blue and white tile patterns, and an inviting bar if additional margaritas feature on your 'to-do' list for the day.

Food 8, Service 8, Atmosphere 8

Taverna Opa *(top)*
36 Ocean Drive (1st St),
South Beach
Tel: 305 673 6730
www.tavernaoparestaurant.com
Open: daily, 4pm 'until the ouzo runs out'
(about 4am)
$45 *Greek*

Taverna Opa is the South Beach Greek fest where locals go to give their Miami Beach poker faces a night off and let their hair down for some ouzo-fuelled crockery-smashing and table-dancing therapy. The menu is mostly all about lamb; lamb shank, fire-roasted lamb and lamb chops are all available, while there is also an assortment of grilled seafood for those sick of lamb. It's an

ideal place to take a group of friends; the Greek flags and paintings create that authentic Hellenic party feeling, while the tables are dressed minimally, allowing easy access to the table-tops for when the music is turned up. For this reason, women are advised not to wear high heels.

Food 7, Service 8, Atmosphere 7

Versailles *(bottom)*
3555 SW 8th Street (SW 36th Ave),
Downtown
Tel: 305 444 0240
Open: daily, 8am–1am
(3am Fri, 4am Sat)
$30 *Cuban*

How did a Cuban tradition get to be called Versailles? Beats us. Regardless, this is the place where the country's immigrants come to reminisce when mama isn't around or when they don't feel like slaving over a stove for five hours. In terms of décor, they're aiming for the palace look, with huge chandeliers and etched mirrors covering almost every surface. However, in reality, the effect is one of a glorified diner, circa 1989. Luckily, the cost of your meal is similarly retro, and portions are, in a word, huge. If you're hard-pressed to take your pick from the substantial menu, just peer over to the other tables and indicate to the waiting staff that's what you'd like, or instead ask for a recommendation. Fortify yourself with a cortadito (strong, short Cuban coffee) for the journey home, and remember to stop at the take-out adjunct at the front for a pastelito or three.

Food 7, Service 8, Atmosphere 7

eat...

Wish

(top)

The Hotel, 801 Collins Avenue (8th St), South Beach
Tel: 305 674 9474
www.wishrestaurant.com
Open: 7am–3pm, 7–10pm (midnight Fri/Sat)

$85 *Modern American*

Located on the premises of the Hotel, Wish's design scheme was orchestrated by fashion designer/décor guru/TV personality Todd Oldham, who also decorated The Hotel's interior. He has created a seemingly private dining patio in tropical blues and greens, the romance factor boosted considerably by a forest of palm trees and exotic plants (the whole scheme was refreshed for the property's tenth anniversary in 2010). Executive chef Marco Ferraro, who trained in the kitchens of Jean-Georges Vongerichten, arrived in 2008. His wordy menu includes such seemingly improbable descriptions as 'grilled Maine lobster tail, local pea tendrils, basil, garlic, ginger, dried finger chillies, lemon-coriander crema, pineapple-jicama salsa' and 'seared foie-gras, blackberry compote, wasabi, white chocolate, almond crumbs'. This is not as disconcerting as it sounds. It's a super option for 'date night', as the dining noise level is considerably lower than at other SoBe spots. After dinner (or before) it would be a shame to miss out on Wish's speciality: 'electronic' cocktails, which are lit up by floating neon ice cubes. This is very Miami, and a bit whimsical, but who says dinner has to be so serious?

Food 9, Service 10, Atmosphere 8

The Villa

(bottom)

by Barton G.

1101 Ocean Drive (11th St), South Beach
Tel: 305 576 8003
www.thevillabybartong.com
Open: 7–10pm (midnight Fri/Sat)

$175 *Modern American*

The Villa by Barton G. opened in March 2010 after Barton G. Weiss turned a stint with Casa Casuarina's current owner Peter Lofti into a deal to establish and oversee a hotel and restaurant – how's that for career advancement for someone who expected to retire 15 years ago? Mr. Weiss' hand here is much more careful than at his namesake restaurant; consider this the multi-part classical concerto to Barton G.'s rock opera prelude. Much like the property it's housed in, the focus at the restaurant is really on impeccable service. Each diner at the table is served simultaneously by a team; your silverware is replaced about two dozen times during your meal; and the head waiter for the ten tables is polished and charming. In short, your wish is their command. The culinary experience is mostly centred on classic preparations (Wagyu beef with Madeira glaze, tea-smoked squab, a perfectly seared Ahi tuna starter) with the occasional dramatic touch (such as the frozen Caesar salad, where the dressing arrives smoking from its liquid nitrogen bath and proceeds to warm up and coat the greens). Given the sumptuous setting, you may be pleasantly surprised when the final bill is presented to you in its cream-colored envelope.

Food 9, Service 10, Atmosphere 9

Zuma (top)

*Hotel Epic, 270 Biscayne
Boulevard Way (Brickell), Downtown
Tel: 305 577 0277
www.zumarestaurant.com
Open: noon–3pm, 6pm–
midnight. Closed Sun*

$57 *Japanese*

In Japanese culture, the *izakaya* is a stepping stone between bar and restaurant,
serving a more substantial repertoire of
food and snacks than a typical drinking
establishment but lacking the full menu
and full-service component of a regular
eatery. We're sure few *izakayas* in Greater
Tokyo resemble Zuma, the statuesque
buxom model in a population of artistically and vertically challenged Japanese
dining spots. The soaring main room was
designed by interior designer Noriyo-
shi Muramatsu, and garbed in the same
earth-tone palette as its Zuma sisters in
London, Dubai, Hong Kong and Istanbul.
The menu, consisting of tempura, cold
dishes, sushi and signature dishes, is a bit
haphazard, and plates arrive when the
kitchen is done preparing them as opposed to when you want them to. However, the 'authentic but not traditional' flavours on display are exciting. Standouts
include the spicy beef tenderloin and the
azami yaki option from the robata (char-
coal grill) section.

Food 9, Service 8, Atmosphere 8

Miami Dining: What's Really Going On?

The dining landscape is quite changed from the mid-2000s when museum-ready, perfectly composed plates – with AA-ticket price tags – were all the rage. Several trends took off since then that are interesting in their own right, but it remains to be seen how much long-term weight they'll have.

eat...

The movement with the greatest potential is the lure of Midtown and the Design District as a dining 'destination'. It started with Michael's Genuine Food & Drink, then Miami's award-winning native chef Michelle Bernstein introduced Sra. Martinez. Since then, Sugarcane, Mercadito and Morgan's have joined the roster of restaurants bringing some gravity to what was previously a dining wasteland.

Direct from Los Angeles, California – with a detour through New York and exposure via cable television's Food Channel – come the food trucks. Rather than sausages cooked in dirty water and sloppy meat patties, however, these mobile foodstands present a gourmet-ish take on casual dining, (okay, Yellow Submarine offers sandwiches and hot dogs, and there's grilled cheese plus from Ms. Cheezious, but we're not complaining). So far, the trucks – each has gained quite a following in Downtown and the districts much further afield – haven't made an impact on South Beach (could be due to licensing restrictions or the somewhat narrow roadways), but the possibilities are huge. Look for Latin House Grill, gastropod, Dim Ssam a Go Go, the Fish Box and Sugar Rush (for dessert), among others, on Twitter to decipher truck locations and hours for any given day.

A similar theme figures into Miami's new fascination with casual 'finer' dining. Recent months have witnessed the debut of no less than three casual-yet-respectable Asian spaces: American Noodle Bar (from former Wish chef Michael Bloise); Gigi ("noodles/bbq/beer") helmed by a Top Chef-testant previously seen at the Ritz-Carlton's DiLido Beach Club; and Sakaya Kitchen (since the proprietors also operate the Dim Ssam a Go Go truck, they're doubly influential). Add the aforementioned Mercadito's Mexican favorites and Sugarcane's tapas/robataya/small-plate mantra to the list, and this is definitely a movement. Is it due to the endless recession and the resultant shrinking of household means or just an attempt to inject a little fun and humor into Miami's always-serious-and-overly-aspiring dining arena? Will we still be talking about these directions (and these venues) next year? You'll have to wait a few months and return….and return…and return again to find out.

drink

It's an unwritten law, which everyone is well aware of; drinking in Miami follows the same rules as eating and sleeping. You must look a million dollars and sup with the utmost elegance, while appearing not to care that charging hundreds of dollars on bottles and cocktails to your credit card is going to really, really hurt in the long run. Any hotel with aspirations has capitalised on this prescription by doing its best to create a destination bar (the idea is meant to appeal to the tourist who says, 'If I can't stay there, I might as well be seen drinking there'). Sometimes the results are tragic. But in other cases the success of some hotel bars has surpassed that of the actual hotel becoming the real star draw.

We've included a few of these in this section (M-Bar and Sky Bar, together with the more approachable Spire Bar and The Bar at Level 25), but there are loads of other drinking holes just waiting to be found. The Setai has a decadently designed Indonesian-influenced courtyard where you can sip Cabernet and pick at Asian street snacks, while the Raleigh has the Martini Bar, an authentic, weathered room that Details magazine named one of the top ten bars in the world. The National has Aquabar by its sleek and spectacular pool, which you arrive at by passing under a gorgeous mosaic on the ceiling of its Tamara restaurant. Guests of the Whitelaw or the Catalina – both overseen by the South Beach Hotel Group – are treated to complimentary cocktails for an hour from 7pm (yes, it's early, but free is free).

Some visitors are smart enough to seek something outside the usual scene, a neat discovery that they can tell their friends about. None of these entries are quite that place, although The Room comes close. This cosy hideout on the sleepier end of South Beach is where you might go for a something a little more low-key and funky. For no-holds-barred places to get hammered, Automatic Slims and Purdy Lounge top the range; at both, cocktails, slammers and shooters are the order of the day. Both are high-octane, testosterone-fuelled binge-drinking destinations where total oblivion – if you want it – is all but guaranteed. Miami's top dive bar is Club Deuce on 14th Street, although this could prove to be a little too much of a dive bar initiation for some of SoBe's scenesters.

Stepping up into the slightly underground (but very trendy section) is Buck 15 – a hip, converted loft space filled with old sofas found in flea markets. Alternatively, think of Rok Bar as the anti-Buck 15, what a pseudo-dive bar might look like if it suddenly inherited a few million dollars. It's two steps up from any other watering hole on the Miami scene, and is still packed every night of the week.

A total 180° from there, Jazid on Washington Avenue is the spot for live music, and always has talented (and occasionally not-so-talented) musicians sweating it out

in its cramped bar area. Also ultra-casual are the Abbey and Transit Lounge, two establishments where it is possible to show up in scruffy attire to extol the merits of a pint and not be outright ridiculed.

The bar stop can serve many purposes; beach interlude, before-dinner palate-opener, post-meal time-killer, pre-club warm-up or after-hours comedown (and there's always the morning-after ramp-up). And since you're in Miami, where drinking is a time-honoured tradition, the means to address any of those situations is likely to be within 50 feet of where you're standing.

The Abbey (left)
1115 16th Street (Lincoln),
South Beach
Tel: 305 538 8110
Open: daily, 11am–5am

How has a dark secret like The Abbey survived all these years? It's probably strictly through word of mouth, since this is as untrendy as it gets (see also Club Deuce). The bar attracts a friendly local following and the odd tourist in similar measure, who are enticed by a handful of Ray Rigazio's IPAs, stouts and lagers (brewed upstate in Melbourne, Florida), and ten others on tap, with a sizeable selection of bottles. As the perfect anti-Miami experience, there's not much to the décor – call it Olde Englishe Pub Light – just some wooden stools and booths, a few modest-sized televisions, a dart board, and a metal beer fridge plastered with stickers. However, if it's dreary outside, you could do worse than quaff a few rounds at the convivial Abbey. The pints are malty and cold, the atmosphere is inviting, and the wizened bartenders who've been around the block a few times would love to tell you their life stories.

Automatic Slims (bottom)
1216 Washington Avenue
(12th St), South Beach
Tel: 305 672 2220
Open: 9pm–5am Mon–Sat

Ah, Automatic Slims, how do your adherents love you? Let us count the ways! 1) the liberal use of neon and 60s-era truck spot/junkyard/bowling alley signage is lots of fun; 2) a rock 'n' roll soundtrack that lifts from the biggest names in 80s hair metal and 00s Ozzfest rosters; 3) oh yes, the naughty girls strutting on the bar in fishnets ('hot rod babes') offering shots from test tubes and pouring them down your throat never gets old; and, finally 4) the effect on the contents of your wallet, which is a slower and more subtle drain than in 85 per cent of the bars on the Beach. Because of such, Automatic Slims attracts a young, game crowd, many of whom are beautiful enough to get into Mansion, but who prefer to hear Guns'n'Roses and slam tequila shots at the bar. There is often no cover charge and the drinks are reasonably priced for Miami. On Tuesdays beer selections and kamikaze shots are $3, and on Thursdays it's Ladies' Night when the girls drink for free until midnight. The drink menu, as it were, is divided into beers, bottles, and 'sissy drinks', which sums things up rather nicely.

Bahia (right)
Four Seasons, 1435 Brickell
Avenue (SE 14th Ln), Downtown
Tel: 305 358 3535
www.fourseasons.com
Open: daily, 11am–6pm

Bahia, located beside the hotel's pool area, is a city slickers' bar with attitude, the first stop for yuppies and career girls just off work and where other pretty people go to meet each other. You can choose from high chairs along an impeccably kept stainless-steel bar or wicker chairs at wooden tables, and there's a snazzy waterfall feature as a backdrop. Most people hover some-

where between the two and peer out towards Biscayne Bay, which separates the Financial District and South Beach. Drinks are priced on the Upper East Side, but luckily there is a bank in the building. If you are in Miami on business, then Bahia is a suitable place to forget or prepare for a meeting, depending on your work ethic.

....

Bar 721 *(top)*
721 N Lincoln Lane (Euclid),
South Beach
Tel: 305 532 1342 www.bar721.com
Open: daily, 5pm–5am

The swanky feel of a luxe lounge without the associated snooty attitude is what you'll find at Bar 721, a relative newcomer to the north end of South Beach. The mood has been captured with some expensive-looking upholstered furniture (those ratty sofas at Purdy Lounge wouldn't fit in here), a few votives and the warmth of the staff who deal admirably with the You Call It, We Pour It two-for-one happy hour block from 2 to 9pm. Minorly tweaked classics (Planter's Punch, Moscow Mule) and new recipes (Ciroc Caribbean) fill up the liquid menu; at $12 per glass, drinks are a relative bargain, especially since there's generally no cover charge. There is also reasonably priced bottle service available, but this is not the place to whip out your Black Amex – you'll appear vulgar. Video jockeys do their best to promote looseness, though a discreetly placed pool table in the back takes up what would normally be a dance floor. No matter, you can boogie among the couches and not miss a beat.

The Bar at Level 25 *(middle)*
Conrad Miami, 1395 Brickell
Avenue (SE 14th St), Downtown
Tel: 305 503 6500
Open: daily, 6.30am–11pm

It's a bit of a shame that this lounge doesn't have a more distinguished moniker, because the experience truly warrants one. This particular lobby bar perches on the 25th floor of the Espirito Santos building, with vistas to die for and seating in a bright lemon colour scheme that displays its mischievous side in earnest. The Bar definitely wants to make an impression, but not in that 'we're too chic for our own good' way easily found elsewhere. Depending on the weekday, happy hour cocktail specials may spotlight wines (50 available by the glass), 'skinny' margaritas or caipirinhas, and the lively set of drinkers to be found here is easily engaged. The smart bet is to turn up for 'Elevated Fridays', when everything is half-off from 5pm to 8pm and the crowd is at its most celebratory. Bring your drink out onto the slim veranda, and take care it doesn't go tumbling 300-feet into the bay below.

....

Buck 15 *(bottom)*
707 Lincoln Lane (Euclid),
South Beach
Tel: 305 538 3815 www.buck15.net
Open: 10pm (8pm Fri/Sat)–5am.
Closed Sundays and Mondays.

It bills itself as a 'gallery lounge', but Buck 15 can be far better described as an overground-underground bar, a 70s rec room dressed in artier clothes. The entrance, on a narrowish lane parallel to Lincoln Road, can be reached via a stairway covered in bright graphic murals. The bar area is a sitting room filled with sofas of questionable provenance, with accents provided by street art canvases and skateboards (stuck on the wall) designed by local emerging artists. New pieces are displayed every month, and if you fancy something enough, almost everything can be taken home for a price. The local DJs who spin here make this one of Miami's top retro lounges, an original space where anything goes. Proceedings are casually overlooked by a giant sumo wrestler painted onto the back wall.

Club Deuce   *(top)*
222 14th Street (Collins Ct),
South Beach
Tel: 305 531 6200
Open: daily, 8am–5am

Some Miami locals boast that they don't go out on a Saturday night but instead get up at the crack of dawn on a Sunday and go to the Deuce for the SoBe after-party at 8am. The Deuce, as they fondly call it, is the authentic Miami dive of old – a relic of the day when cocaine and gunshot wounds were as common as sunburn on South Beach – and it is proud to admit it (actually, it is rumoured to be much older than that, with a birth year of 1926). The bar is not pretty, nor are the bartenders, but therein lies its charm. All sorts of people drink at the Deuce. It's a place where strippers, glamour models, and the occasional odd celebrity (Mickey Rourke fits this label) bet their next shot of whisky on the next set of pool table results. So if you don't like

the high-hooch club scene at Miami, put the olive back in your martini glass and head towards the Deuce. Show up during the eleven-hour happy hour (opening until 7pm), order a beer and sit safe in the knowledge that you might end up talking to a transvestite, a Hollywood actor, or a lorry driver from Texas. Here, the possibilities are endless.

Eno's Wine   *(bottom)*
& Tapas Bar
920 Lincoln Road (Jefferson Ave),
South Beach
Tel: 305 695 1119
www.enos-sobe.com
Open: daily, 6pm–2am

Despite its sophisticated reputation, wine is frequently overlooked down here in favour of a lurid shades of sexy-sounding cocktail or hard liquor. Eno's is a great place to kick back with a glass without feeling wine snobs are looking over your shoulder. They have one of those very cool enomatic machines that allow future oenophiles to sample as little as an ounce of vino from a list of 60 bottles from some of the world's great vineyards (no need to do this all in one sitting, however). Eno's also possesses – as it must – a knowledgeable staff, who actively encourage customers to linger and chat about all things viticulture. And the tapas, paninis and charcuterie provide a fine counterpoint to the wine (the entrées are fine, if not particularly memorable). Much of the seating is outdoors fronting the hectic walkway; try to snag one of the dashing blue, red and silver chairs in the centre for maximum photo-op effect.

drink...

Finnegan's Way *(left)*

1344 Ocean Drive (14th St),
South Beach
(also Finnegan's 2 at 942 Lincoln Road)
Tel: 305 672 7747
www.finnegansway.com
Open: daily, 8am–2am

If, after a few sleepless nights on South Beach, the word 'mojito' doesn't have quite the same draw as it used to, chances are Finnegan's Way is your antidote. The bar offers the Irish alternative to Miami, where pints are slurped, sports are viewed, and wings, jalapeno peppers and coconut shrimp are chomped on (pizza, lobster and steak are served, too). Finnegan's is located at the northern end of the Drive, away from most of the tourists, so it can be a welcome resting-post. The outdoor bar is where the action happens, especially in the late afternoon and early evening when Finnegan's fills up, serving as a central station for footie and baseball fans.

Gordon Biersch *(right)*
Brewery

1201 Brickell Avenue (SE 12th St), Miami
Tel: 786 425 1130
www.gordonbiersch.com
Open: daily, 11.30am–11pm

Gordon Biersch Brewery is located in Miami's financial district, a block away from the Conrad Hotel and the Four Seasons. The convivial brew pub (German lager is their game) fills up with businessmen ready to let off steam after work, and is often the setting for a fiery round of business card exchanges. The abundance of television screens means that Gordon Biersch also heats up depending on the local sporting contests. This is predominantly a restaurant – think steaks, chicken parm, planked salmon – but the bar stools and mingling space help keep things hopping. Generally, visitors won't think of Gordon Biersch as anything more than an enjoyable time-waster. A pint here will not result in an evening of drunkenness or random hook-ups.

Jazid *(bottom)*

1342 Washington Avenue (14th St),
South Beach
Tel: 305 673 9372
www.jazid.net
Open: daily, 10pm–5am

Originally, the idea was to entice South Beach's nocturnal warriors with a spot of jazz. But South Beach is not the kind of place where the masses, pretensions notwithstanding, sit down and savour the sounds of trumpets, saxophones and pianos. So though there are occasional jazz sessions, you're much more likely to be treated to a spot of reggae (Fridays and Sundays) or 'Latin alternative' at this longstanding performance bar (check out the extensive calendar on their website). Patrons are happy to pile into Jazid's cramped red-lit interior and guzzle up the beer, vodka and live music. Acid house, R&B and hip-hop emanate from the upstairs DJ lounge with a pool table and cocktail bar, but the main stage events are downstairs where performances start at 9pm. Dress code at Jazid is casual, so tanktops and jeans are acceptable. There is a cover charge of $10 on the weekends, but if

111

you look confident at the door then the doorman may let you off paying.

....

M-Bar *(left)*
*Mandarin Oriental, 500
Brickell Key Drive, Downtown
Tel: 305 913 8288
www.mandarinoriental.com
Open: daily, 5pm–midnight (1am Fri/Sat)*

The bar here is topped with Blue Bahia, which is supposedly the finest, most expensive marble on the planet. Not quite as expensive, but easily more impressive are floor-to-ceiling windows that expose panoramic views of Biscayne Bay and the Miami skyline. M-Bar attracts Miami's business in-crowd, those who love their suits and those who like to dress up after a hard day at the beach and pretend they have been chained to a desk all day. Although the days of martini lunches are long gone, part of the appeal at M-Bar is the 250 varieties of martini shaken and stirred by the bar staff – sweet, tangy, 'naughty but nice'(?) and odd-ball options, including tipples aimed at James Bond and Frank Sinatra fans, coffee-lovers and drinkers who can't live without black pepper. The party on Friday evenings has become a familiar cog in the Miami party circuit. M-Bar opens at 5pm and serves sushi nibbles for those who don't have the time to invest in a proper dinner before their next series of bar hops.

....

Monty's *(top)*
*300 Alton Road (2nd St),
South Beach
Tel: 305 672 1148
www.montyssobe.com*

*Open: daily, 11am–10.30pm
(11pm Fri/Sat)*

While Monty's is not much to look at, it does have its positives. It is the only bar that overlooks the South Beach marina, so in your alcohol-induced haze you can imagine what it's like to own one of the powerboats moored in front of you. The poolside bar and outside tables sit below a Caribbean-style thatched palm roof, while the large indoor space is accented with sea nets and various maritime thingies. Don't be tempted to swim in the pool, as all sorts of things, including cocktails and intoxicated birthday boys, are thrown in after dark. Monty's attracts the kind of weekend drinker that likes to start early, so a Thursday or Friday evening is the best time to see Monty's in full flow. For that matter, it also attracts the weekday early drinker (and others who are just up for a killer deal), since Monty's happy 'hour' lasts for four of them (starting at 4pm daily). Fish dishes and an oyster, clam and shrimp raw bar figure into the scene, but the menu items have only a modest fan base. This is a suitable place for a sip after a scuba-diving or fishing trip – you can brag all you want without annoying serious drinkers.

....

Mova *(right)*
*1625 Michigan Avenue
(Lincoln Ln S), South Beach
Tel: 305 534 8181
www.movalounge.com
Open: daily, 3pm–3am*

Like many of Miami's partymakers, this gay lounge is at once sleek and somewhat larger than advertised. The walls

drink...

of the former Halo are all white but textured, so the mood lighting, evolving from oranges to pinks, gets to produce horizontal shadowing that sets off the stylish local crowd. Most of the activity (swallowing large quantities of tropic-coloured cocktails) takes place around the bar, but a few cushioned white benches with decorative pillows line the edges of the room. The crowd can range from the subdued to the chatty, depending on the time of day, the evening's program and your luck, so you may want to send in a scout.

Palace (left)
1200 Ocean Drive (12th St),
South Beach
Tel: 305 531 7234
Open: daily, 10am–midnight

You can't miss Palace on Ocean Drive. Not because the gay community's multicoloured striped flag flutters beside the bar or a chattering all-male group occuping the open-fronted bar area, but because during the day it is normally the most jolly place on Ocean Drive. Plop yourself on one of the metallic stools on the raised level of the bar and watch the people walk by or grab one the tables and stools on the pavement (watch out for stray rollerbladers!). The Palace is the only place for drag on Ocean Drive; the bar puts on shows Friday and Saturday at 6 or 7pm, and you can have your omelette with a side of fabulosity during the two Sunday 'Brunchic' sessions (note: Miami is suspiciously void of cleverly-named drag performers – shouldn't Gusty Winds reside in Florida?). And if you fancy some water sports afterwards

(day or night), the gay section of the beach is located dead ahead.

Purdy Lounge (bottom)
1811 Purdy Avenue (18th St),
South Beach
Tel: 305 531 4622
www.purdylounge.com
Open: daily, 3pm (6pm Sat/Sun)–5am

It's almost worth getting in a taxi just to watch the surfing videos projected onto the big screens at Purdy Lounge, otherwise lit by low-slung aluminium lamps hanging from the ceiling. Despite its bohemian vibe, Purdy Lounge is always busy and the atmosphere is rather like that of an upscale frat-house, with a laid-back, fun-loving party crowd that skews a bit local. The front room is ringed up top with lava lamps, and on the ground with comfortable armchairs and couches that have seen better days. You can also shoot pool on a table that sits beneath some framed portraits (these appear to be inspired by Lego blocks and impart a strangely sinister air). Also check out the rear lounge, dubbed the Scarface room. The barmen are chilled, the drinks are strong, and like most serious entertainment establishments in Miami, the doors are open until 5am.

RokBar (right)
1905 Collins Avenue
(20th St), South Beach
Tel: 305 674 4397
www.rokbarmiami.com
Open: 11pm–5am Tues–Sat

Veteran rocker Tommy Lee had a hand in opening RokBar in 2004, and if he's nowhere to be seen today, at least his imprint is still in evidence aurally (and probably in spirit in other ways as well – the red leather hearts in the women's bathroom?). RokBar – so much more than just a bar – is pretty much a safe bet in the nightlife badlands of Miami. It's like a retro mini Studio 54 with rotating lights on the ceiling, iron crosses set into the black leather walls and giant rock-chick hero figures lit up behind the bar. The tall pair of blonde bartenders dressed in tiny shredded outfits are the most popular figures in the house, and serve drinks with a side portion of attitude. The DJ is well-educated in all genres and can segue from Ke$ha to Ozzy Osbourne effortlessly. Entrance is free, but an early arrival is paramount because this place fills up quickly after midnight, especially as the Mynt doormen next door become more arrogant. Tables can be booked, but the small lounge area towards the entrance is only really used by people who are about to pass out.

The Room (top)
100 Collins Avenue
(entrance on 1st Street
between Collins and Washington
Avenue), South Beach
Tel: 305 531 6061
Open: daily, 6pm–5am

The evening light, and later on, the candles on the bar, transform an otherwise pedestrian spot into a cosy nook where couples (and perfect strangers!) feel free enough to initiate spontaneous make-out sessions. Such is the power of The Room, a bar surrounded by a collection of high tables and floppy sofas that draw a friendly, predominantly local clientele. As its nondescript name may suggest, the bar is whatever you want it to be. From 6pm onwards hairdressers, businessmen and photographers sip on continental lager and Yorkshire brown ale, and MB visitors stop in for a before-dinner glass of wine. Subsequent waves may arrive at 10pm (after dinner) or midnight (for pre-club warm-up). Later on, the Room brims with additional waitresses and patrons from the restaurants around the corner (Prime One Twelve, Shohi Sushi), with some stragglers that arrive as the clubs up-beach thin out. The blackboard above the bar spells out the wide-ranging selection of beer (around 70 different drafts and bottles) and wine, and there's not a cocktail shaker to be found. It is not often that you find a secret location in Miami like The Room, but it is a pleasure when it does happen.

Rose Bar (bottom)
Delano Hotel, 1685 Collins
Avenue (17th St), South Beach
Tel: 305 674 6400
www.delanohotelmiami.com
Open: daily, noon–2am (3am Fri/Sat)

A trip to the Rose Bar is an enjoyable way to see exactly why the Delano was such a sensation on its debut. Indeed, the hotel's in-house bar is a stylish sidekick to the Delano's towering lobby, but it's really no more than a long deep-set alcove cleverly lit and blending in with the lobby's theme park-like setting. This is an inviting place to sit on cushioned stools or play a frame of pool, if the models let you; the coin-on-the-table reserva-

drink...

tion technique does not seem to work with them. But sometimes it's best to sit back and let them show you how the game should be played. Rose Bar still attracts an interesting crowd – ignore anyone who says otherwise. The cocktails are as strong and as expensive as ever.

***

Safari Bar (top)
Chesterfield Hotel, 855 Collins Avenue (9th St), South Beach
Tel: 305 531 5831
www.thechesterfieldhotel.com
Open: daily, 7am–1am

Underneath the disapproving eyes of a few stuffed antelopes, one can down a few glasses of something killer at Safari Bar. Here, you're as likely to see candied, adolescent options (Chocolate Cake, Surfer on Acid, Buttery Nipple) as you are the harder stuff and Champagne on the drinks menu. And the vibe is both easy and casual, as the bar takes up a corner of the Chesterfield Hotel that's costumed to seem more expansive than it is. Cowhide-covered seating is posed under a mirror, where those in transit (one way or another) sip and pout. If you crave exposure, relax on the terrace and let yourself be entertained by the cars driving slowly past to show off their spoilers, or by the women that strut past having just spent a wad of their husbands hard-earned cash in the nearby boutiques. This is a perfect spot for a pre-dinner drink on the armless white leather sofas near the bar. If they're all occupied, head down the road to the Whitelaw Hotel, which has the same owner and the same vibe.

If you don't like armless white leather sofas, then you are in the wrong town.

***

Sky Bar (bottom)
The Shore Club, 1901 Collins Avenue (20th St), South Beach
Tel: 305 695 3100
www.shoreclub.com
Open: daily, 7pm–2am

A series of carefully constructed indoor and outdoor settings conspire to form Sky Bar, one of the Shore Club's top draws and a mainstay of the South Beach social tableau. The four areas – Redroom, Redroom Garden, and the more intimate Sandbar and Rumbar, with 75 versions of the eponymous spirit available – are connected by a chain of leafy garden mazes, and each has cosy alcove sections, secret passages and separate-yet-interlocking moods. Around midnight, the activity gravitates toward Redroom with its North Africa-meets-the Hamptons vibe and Moroccan-style lanterns for lighting flavour. Some would say that the beautiful people congregate here, but others judge the clientele as more intriguing than breathtaking; regardless of which camp you belong to your fellow drinkers are remarkably friendly, not always a given on SoBe. Sky Bar and its velvet ropes have always connoted an air of exclusivity. That hasn't changed, but it is a bit less exclusive than it used to be. It is open to hotel guests and the public at large, but the party police at the door do exercise a selective door policy (there's never a cover, but a table reservation with a minimum spend per person will guarantee entry).

drink…

Spire Bar *(bottom)*

The Hotel, 801 Collins Avenue (8th St), South Beach
Tel: 305 531 2222
www.thehotelofsouthbeach.com
Open: sunset–midnight Thurs–Sat

The spire in question owes its classy rep to a famous jeweller, and this bar is one of the hidden gems of the Beach. In 1998 Tiffany & Co. (of the robin's-egg-blue box) challenged what was the Tiffany Hotel over the rights to its name. Never mind that the hotel had opened 59 years earlier; Tiffany the retailer was victorious, but the hotel was allowed to keep the famous Tiffany Spire on the roof of the building. After a period of collective masterminding, developer Tony Goldman and his team renamed the hotel The Hotel. They also smartly fitted a bar at the base of the spire and added some red, lilac and grey flooring and white-pillowed deck furniture to make this a casual but special atmosphere from which to watch the sun sink. With views of the entire city, this has to be one of the most idyllic spots to soak in the South Beach experience. The bar hosts Thursday night parties, and there is access to the Hotel's roof pool, also lit up at night, if one needs to get away for even more intimate conversation.

Tequila Chicas *(left)*

1501 Ocean Drive (15th St), South Beach
Tel: 305 531 7010
Open: daily, 11am–4am

Only a short walk from the beach, Tequila Chicas is a Latin bar in an artsy courtyard at the northern tip of Ocean Drive. It's a dog-eat-dog world in Miami, so at Tequila Chicas they offer some staggering deals on drinks to draw the customers in. The bar itself is a solid, square structure built in stone and topped with wooden surfaces, decorated with baskets full of limes and a blonde bartender who crushes the fruit and grinds the mint. The mood can only be described as tropical and unpretentious. The bar fills in the early evenings as the local daytime restaurant crews get off work and people make their way back from the beach. Tequila Chicas is at its best for futbol contests or major televised sporting events. Not so chic, but once the firewater starts flowing, everything looks a bit better.

Transit Lounge *(right)*

729 SW 1st Avenue (SW 8th St), Downtown
Tel: 305 377 4628
www.transitlounge.us
Open: daily, 5pm (8pm Fri–Sun)–5am

Situated, perhaps appropriately, on the other side of the tracks, Transit Lounge is a favourite among locals who like to throw back in a large, unfancy space where the bartenders don't sneer at you for ordering a cheap-ass beer. Outfitted with a pool table and some two-tops beneath bright portraits of rock royalty, the dark room has mastered that lived-in feeling of all great drinking establishments that have stood the test of time. The commanding wooden bar itself is nicely worn, and the two-for-one happy hour weekdays from 5 to 8pm draws drinkers like a shoofly pie draws flies.

Another reason to dive in is the varied roster of live performances, which take place every night aside from Mondays when Rock Band 3 pretenders take to the stage. Now's the time to debut your air guitar skills on the road, and pound the brews after.

Vue/Passage Bar *(bottom)*
Hotel Victor, 1144 Ocean Drive (12th St), Miami Beach
Tel: 305 428 1234
www.hotelvictorsouthbeach.com
Open: daily, 5pm–midnight

An undulating brown and cream-striped canopy overhead might trick you into thinking you're in the Sahara – but miles of sand are only to be found back on the beach. In any case, these two connected areas adjacent to the pool and sun deck function as an all-day respite from the hubbub of the outside world beyond the hotel walls. In the afternoon, when food is on offer, a panini or the steak and pineapple salad with a side of truffle fries works wonders in soaking up the alcohol; in the evening, a drink here is cooling after a scorching day on the beach. The place is seductively lit, the music is kept to a good volume and the breeze is soothing. The bar closes early compared to its counterparts elsewhere, so think of this as a first stop.

Enough With Bottle Service
– Can I Just Have a Beer, Please?

Yes, Miami drinkers are a bit strange in their habits. Where else would the hottest place to down inebriating beverages of any kind be… a parking garage? (It's spectacular, naturally.) Alas, as of this writing, the structure at 1111 Lincoln Road is only an event space, and not a full-on drinking establishment…but it's probably only a matter of time.

One can't help but think that everyone who visits the city is on a giant bender, one that lasts the entire time they're here. Liquor isn't just everywhere; it's often the main topic of concern. It's mentioned even in situations that would normally preclude its consideration (see: breakfast). Even away from Ocean Drive, Washington and Collins, alcohol rules. All the non-beach social activity is usually centered on hard alcohol (as with the overpriced bottle service) and mixed drinks, with the mojito, martini and the sweet umbrella drink cast as the liquid equivalent of Mafia family heads.

Yet, there is room in Miami for drinkers of beer and wine. You may have to look a little deeper for a venue of choice, but a fan of the golden beverage does have options. Among others, this book includes The Abbey (decidedly casual yet deadly beer-serious) and Gordon Biersch (a somewhat corporate take on the brew pub). The football hooligan can opt for Finnegan's Way (or Finnegan's 2) or the eau-de-frathouse-fragrant Playright on Washington, or Hofbrau on Lincoln Road, depending on where one's sporting sympathies lie. Any connoisseur would do well to check out 'The Room', where the six dozen tap and bottled selections consist of Americans and a healthy Belgian contingent along with representatives from the Caribbean, Germany, Japan, Scotland and Canada.

For oenophiles, it's trickier to find quality offerings; upper-end restaurants are often good bets. Probably the most notable ones can be found, with a little perseverance, on Lincoln Road in the form of Eno's (a cafe and store with 60 labels available by the glass and close to a thousand more in stock) and Meat Market (which has to maintain its heady wine list of 350 international varieties to stand up to all that meat). In the heart of South Beach, The Setai and Prime One Twelve (with its attractive brick-backed bar) are standout spots, as are The River and the Four Seasons in Downtown . With all the players here, champagne is more readily available (and more highly priced) than in other major cities. If you're feeling romantic, without a doubt the best place to count the tiny bubbles in a romantic setting is the Spire Bar at sunset. If you're not looking for an amorous evening, The Bar at Level 25 will certainly fulfill your requirements – and there are always hotel guests buzzing about if you change your mind.

drink…

snack...

All too often, a city's snacking scene is an afterthought, its execution both sloppy and random. It's a spur of the moment decision – subject to factors of sleep-deprivation, intoxication and/or sunstroke – that usually results in either a spin through the nearest Golden Arches or a mad dash through the aisles of a large Walgreen's drugstore, bypassing (for once) the booze and healthier items and seizing upon a prepared sandwich or a nasty pastry sweating in cellophane.

Which is a shame, since Miami holds more than a few stops that are sympathetic to your purse strings, your double-booked schedule and your trendy sensibilities. High up on the list, style-wise, are Morgan's, Fontana and the Icebox Café. The first is a kind of tasty oasis amidst some of the Design District's most unadorned blocks. When in Coral Gables, the Biltmore Hotel is a must, and its restaurant, Fontana, in a shaded courtyard, is the perfect antidote to a hectic lifestyle (although a lunch beside the Biltmore's epic-sized pool, with statues of gods and goddesses looking on, is undoubtedly sexier). Finally, the Icebox Café concocts dozens of sumptuous cakes, and both delicious and daring (for a bakery) lunch and dinner entrées.

Much more casual are classic diners such as 11th Street and Jerry's Famous Deli, where you can grab breakfast or a full meal literally any time day or night. At each, pages upon pages of classic Americana await, filled with dishes adopted from all over the globe (those of an indecisive nature, stay away). If it's your first time in the U.S., this is a good way to approach typical American excess. David's Café, in central South Beach, is similar in soul but with an all-Cuban roster. These are perhaps best experienced in the wee hours, when the most colourful cast of characters shows up.

In between are the Ocean Drive spots where it's common (with the cooperation of your server) to spend up to 90 minutes eating, discussing trivial topics and spying on pedestrians with cameras and beachgoers in skimpy attire. Cardozo and the Pelican Café are prime examples, and the simultaneously busy, but calming, News Café is also worth a look.

Though you'll run into one or two 'official' fast food joints in Miami Beach, there are two that bring the game to new heights. Shake Shack, a New York City import, makes burgers that taste better than the ones you grill at home, though with the queue and the cooking time they don't quite qualify as fast food. Then there's Pasha's, a comely, casual sit-down affair (with an appropriately Miami-esque interior) that pushes Middle Eastern street food towards respectability.

When they say Miami is a city that never sleeps, they also mean that it's a place you can always find something to eat, no matter what time it is.

11th Street Diner *(top)*

1065 Washington Avenue (11th St),
South Beach
www.eleventhstreetdiner.com
Tel: 305 534 6373
Open: daily, 7am–midnight Mon–
Wed, 24 hours Thurs–Sun

This classic American diner was up-rooted from its original home in Wilkes-Barre, Pennsylvania, in 1948 and reassembled on South Beach. It landed, in all its blingy Airstream glory, right beside what is now Twist, and serves every kind of comfort food imaginable. Due to its prime location smack-bang in the middle of Clubland Central, it's guaranteed that the customers at 3am on a Sunday will consist of a combination of the following: an intoxicated and quite boisterous pack of not-quite-young-anymore ladies down from Philly for the weekend, dating couples in their highest couture coming off four hours of trance music at B.E.D., and insomniacs who have nothing better to do than eat. Like Jerry's Famous Deli, it's open all day every day, but it's smaller, the staff are friendlier and the food cheaper. 11th St Diner is a good place for a hungover breakfast on the way to the beach.

A La Folie *(middle)*

516 Española Way (Drexel),
South Beach
Tel: 305 538 4484
www.alafoliecafe.com
Open: daily, 9am–midnight

So you turned left onto Española Way and found yourself on the Left Bank? The smell of croissants and the softly murmured 'ouis' signify that, yes, this establishment on a lane named for Spain is French in flavour. Locals have enjoyed the authentic feel of the café in such reliable numbers the owners opened a twin on Sunset Harbor Drive on the west side of town. The stuffed crêpes, savoury or sweet, make for a perfect breakfast or diet-friendly lunch (the Dijonnaise and the Bordaloue are among the top offerings, but choose a salad or baguette sandwich if you prefer). Don't forget the coffee, which is heavenly. This cosy bistro allows a nice respite from the de rigeur hipness factor of every other Miami Beach dining spot, but be warned that the service regularly borders on glacial. Even better, it's a great deal, since 98 per cent of the menu items are less than $10. While it may not be a destination in and of itself, A La Folie provides a pleasant enough break between bouts of obsessive spending at the nearby clothing shops.

American Noodle Bar *(bottom)*

6730 Biscayne Boulevard
(NE 68th St), North Miami
Tel: 305 396 3269
www.americannoodlebar.com
Open: 11am–11pm Mon–Thurs (1am
Fri/Sat)

Are springy noodles the next foodie frontier? Stop in to American Noodle Bar and cast your vote. Here they're not the ignored section of Column A but a nicely chewy base on which to assemble your dream meal – load up on the add-ons (among them oxtail, deep fried egg, Chinese sausage, garlic pork meatballs) and choose from

snack...

the checklist of sauces (ranging from basil butter through smoked lobster to beef and brown sugar ginger). What you end up with is entirely up to you. Chef and owner Michael Bloise has quite the impressive resume, with noted stints at groundbreakers like Tantra and Wish, and a similarly interesting backstory (he's a native Floridian but his ancestry is Vietnamese-Italian). He's created a hip place that doesn't condescend to its diners. But if any noodle joint could put on airs, this would be the one.

***

Balans *(left)*
1022 Lincoln Road (Lenox),
South Beach
Tel: 305 534 9191
www.balans.co.uk
Open: daily, 8am–midnight (1am Fri/Sat)

Balans is London's representative on the Beach and is regarded by some to be the ideal café and bar. This place fills with an eclectic mix of people, but under the surface the gay community see this as somewhere to meet potential love interests. The staff often behaves as though their agents were about to come through the door waving the next Armani contract, and will pour your club soda absently while staring at their reflection in the mirrors along the interior walls. Balans is fun – if you know what to expect. The menu offers a range of filling recipes with an Asian or Mediterranean twist, while there is a long bar that attracts all sorts in the evening. Balans, suitable for breakfast or lunch, is slightly more sophisticated and less in-your-face than other Lincoln Road hangouts.

Baru Urbano *(right)*
1001 South Miami Avenue
(SE 10th St), Downtown
www.barurbano.com
Tel: 786 991 4570
Open: daily, 11.30am–1am (4am Fri/Sat), 10am–3pm Sun

The frequently boisterous Baru Urbano, in Mary Brickell Village, has the too-studied look of a perfectly cultivated Hard Rock for Caribbean Street Life. However, the business folk and professional shopper customers pay no heed to this, engrossed as they are in their Pan-Latin platters of *picada* and fried yellowtail and their South Miami salads (olives, artichokes, palm hearts and gorgonzola). The menu has been well constructed, and offers possibilities for both committed meat-eaters and vegetarians. Lunch specials during the week are a wallet-friendly $10. Ladies are treated to drink specials and much chatting up on Wednesday nights, and Baru Urbano's happy hours (the best time to sample tacos and *arepitas*) are also well-attended. On Fridays, the tiny, jammed bar overflows with couples and quads who spill over into the back patio, festooned with colourful street-signs.

***

Café Nuvó *(bottom)*
412 Española Way
(Washington), South Beach
Tel: 305 534 5822
www.verestaurants.com
Open: daily, noon–1am (2am Fri/Sat)

Café Nuvó takes up two storefronts, but spilling out onto the sidewalk with its ruined-Gothic-Cuban/Spanish dé-

cor, it would catch the eye of even the most unobservant passer-by. Red wallpaper and patina-layered chandeliers feature on one side, while the other is more casual with old sepia photos and graffiti scribbles. It's more than a little charming, and doesn't quite reek of tourist bait as some of the others on the block do. What you'll find on the menu is Mediterranean in ancestry, but on the whole it ain't particularly expensive. Known for it's extensive list of mojitos, who ever knew there were so many, just as many people come here to drink as to eat. You know when you're in Miami when the restaurant even offers a pet menu, a decidedly odd but quirky welcome touch to the pouty patrons. More substantial fare can be found here, too, but it's just as easy – and cheaper – to take in the café's wonderful atmosphere through a late lunch or a stay at the bar.

....

Cardozo Café *(top)*
1300 Ocean Drive (13th St),
South Beach
Tel: 305 695 2822
Open: daily, 8am–midnight (1am Fri / Sat)

Cardozo Café is located in the Art Deco hotel of the same name, situated at the tranquil northern end of Ocean Drive. Owned by Gloria Estefan, it was built in 1939 by Henry Hohauser and his team who were responsible for much of the look of the area. The Cardozo is a popular spot for breakfast or lunch, as the food here is considerably better than many of its imitators on the stretch – if you are going to spend around $12 for a vegetarian crêpe, you might as well do it at the Cardozo. Alternatively, as on

the rest of Ocean Drive, you can down a quick order of eggs, hash browns and toast for $5, if you do it before 11am. Guests can sit in the hotel's somewhat subdued lobby area, but most opt for outside on one of the wicker chairs or in the shade of the umbrellas that hug the sidewalk. The atmosphere is relaxed until lunchtime, when the place really becomes busy with revellers who have just rolled out of bed, looking for their first margarita of the day.

....

Cavalier Crab Shack *(middle)*
1320 Ocean Drive
(15th St), South Beach
Tel: 305 531 3555
www.cavaliermiami.com
Open: daily, 8.30am–midnight

Architecturally, the Art Deco Cavalier is a gem. Built in 1936 and renovated in 1992, the hotel is best visited with a quick lunch at its charming crab shack. The eatery offers fabulously fresh seafood right on Ocean Drive; expect piled-high plates such as clam chowder, grouper sandwich and conch fritters, all of which can be enjoyed on white-clothed tables on the terrace outside. While you could order food right up to the room, the people-watching opportunities here are too good to miss.

....

David's Café *(bottom)*
1058 Collins Avenue (11th St),
South Beach
Tel: 305 534 8736
www.davidscafe.com
Open: daily, 24 hours

In 1977, Miami and the Beach could most politely be described as 'blighted'. Even so, the Gonzalez family opened up shop on South Beach in the form of a runway-wide Cuban café and take-out window. The place struck a chord with the Caribbean locals, word of mouth brought it to the attention of everyone else, and the family-run David's Café is still here, successful enough to expand into proper premises several years ago. The servers tread back and forth on black and grey mosaic tiles, and place your *bistec palomilla* and *tostones* on tables inlaid with artefacts from the motherland in the form of bills, stamps and postcards. What you see is what you get at David's; a tasty, (almost) home-cooked meal quickly and without artifice. Best of all, potential customers who are too hungover to function or can't leave the cabana are rewarded for calling David's with free delivery anywhere on SoBe.

Fontana *(top)*
Biltmore Hotel, 1200 Anastasia Avenue (Columbus), Coral Gables
Tel: 305 445 8066
www.biltmorehotel.com
Open: daily, 6.30am–10.30pm Mon–Sat, 10am–2pm, 6–10.30pm Sun

Coral Gables should be given credit for some of the best restaurants in Miami, but surprisingly there aren't many places where you can sit outside in the shade and have lunch. Which is why this courtyard, with sunshades arranged around its central fountain, is the most popular lunch spot in the area. Fontana attracts a mixed crowd; tourists who have come to see the ho-

tel, locals who are rich enough to take the afternoon off for some pampering at the spa, and, of course, golfers fresh from a round on the Biltmore's championship course. Don't forget to take a peek at the gigantic pool, which is the most challenging place in Miami to do a length under water. But don't try it after lunch. With its nine different food stations, Sunday brunch is remarkably popular, so book early.

Gigi *(bottom)*
3470 North Miami Avenue (35th St), Design District
Tel: 305 573 1520 www.giginow.com
Open: noon–4pm, 6pm–3am (5am Fri/Sat, 1am Sun).

Drop some Chinese food in a container. Add a generous helping of American Southern soul food. A dash of Thai peanuts and coconut, Indian tandoori, Japanese tempura coating. Blend at high speed. What you'd end up with (in theory) might be something like what you find on the menu here. For example, the menu, broken into categories, with a few dishes in each, including: basics, buns, raw, snack, rice bowl and noodle bowl – sports unlikely bedfellows as short rib meatloaf, raw Florida snapper, teriyaki bok choi, steak and eggs, and Thai basil/avocado/tomato salad. It's all been put together by a former Ritz-Carlton Miami chef, and, since opening, applauded from all directions. This isn't fine dining, but it is as close to a global melting pot as anything down here in the Sun Belt – and nonetheless manages to hold together as its own special entity. Fast food is rarely this brilliant. (And yes, it is delivered to your table in a flash.)

stop here eludes you, you can still enjoy some decadence on the flight home.

Icebox Café *(top)*
1657 Michigan Avenue
(Lincoln Ln N), South Beach
Tel: 305 538 8448
www.iceboxcafe.com
Open: daily, 8am–11pm
(midnight Fri/Sat)

Not long ago, Icebox Café received the American equivalent of the OBE. Media queen Oprah Winfrey proclaimed that it made the "best cakes in the country" (her favourite? The Bomb, a chocolate implosion consisting of layers of dark cake, bittersweet chocolate mousse and cheesecake brownie, all covered in ganache). Royal recommendation notwithstanding, it's not difficult to appreciate these creations; one only needs to taste them. Aside from the aforementioned cakes (20+ varieties), pies and ice-cream sandwiches, the cafe provides an interesting and impressive complement of lunch and dinner entrées (artichoke risotto, curried chicken breast) and a similarly diverse brunch menu on the weekend. The noshing takes place a block or two off active Lincoln Road in a spare yet comfy room, with a few tables, a stainless steel counter and a couple of sofas for those waiting for a hangover cure. Even if you're drooping from the after-effects of alcoholic excess, M (the manager) and Nathan (your server) keep visits here lively and fun with their frisky personalities. An Icebox Café stand recently opened at the new American Airlines wing at MIA, so if a

Jerry's Famous Deli *(bottom)*
1450 Collins Avenue
(Espanola Way), South Beach
Tel: 305 532 8030
www.jerrysfamousdeli.com
Open: daily, 24 hours

It literally takes a hurricane warning to make Jerry's Famous Deli close its doors. During the last serious one a few years ago, the barman waited at the restaurant until the entire population of South Beach had been evacuated before boarding up the windows. Then he went surfing. Open 24 hours a day, Jerry's is, for the most part, a quintessential New York diner, only one that finds itself amongst date palms and year-round heat instead of blaring traffic and bitchy customers. In fact, you may need each of those 24 hours to make a decision, since the menu is as overstuffed as the sandwiches, with an astonishing 600 dishes on the menu. All the famous American classics are in residence – hamburgers and hotdogs, BBQ and melty macaroni and cheese, hot open turkey, apple pie – along with picks from the Middle Eastern, Italian, Mexican and Jewish repertoires. Even a vegetarian can dine well here. There are also some sinful puddings and cheesecakes on display. Prices are a touch high, but this is still fun diner, not fine dining. The high-backed red leather booths are super to relax in for a post-club meal; they've occasionally hosted the odd celeb looking for a decent pastrami sandwich and cherry cola instead of flashbulbs and headlines.

snack...

Joe's Take Out (top)

*11 Washington Avenue
(S Pointe Dr), South Beach
Tel: 305 673 4611
www.joesstonecrab.com
Open: daily, 7.30am–9pm (10pm Fri/
Sat). Closed mid-May to mid-Oct.*

People flock to Joe's Stone Crab restaurant next door purely for the food: it's not the atmosphere or the service that they crave – they are there for the stone crabs. By going to Joe's Take Out you can avoid the hassle of waiting in line for a table with hordes of hungry Florida folk, but you'll still likely have to queue before you can order. There are other items here as well, soups, seafood salads, hot fish entrée platters and sandwiches that you order from various counters and can take to a table with a bottle of wine. In any case, you'll be able to take some delicious stone crabs to the destination of your choice – we recommend the beach at dusk, but a late afternoon snack at your hotel pool is also marvellous. The claws are placed in ice, so they will be fresh for hours.

Kung Fu Kitchen (middle)

*Catalina Hotel, 1700 Collins
Avenue (18th St), South Beach
Tel: 305 534 7905
www.catalinasouthbeach.com
Open: daily, 5pm–midnight
(bar closes 4am)*

The tiny blue pinlights wrapped around the palms make this venue disarmingly attractive at night. Kung Fu Kitchen doesn't show quite as well during the day – much like the majority of the club kids that stop by on their way to Louis – but it's not for lack of trying, and the orange table umbrellas are eye-catching, to say the least. Any item from the full roster of all-over-the-map Asian plates (such as Korean short ribs and Hong Kong steak with shrimp chips) can be had for $20 or less, and a few snappy house maki rolls share the card with more familiar dishes. Saturday's Forbidden City burlesque dinner-show rocks, and Friday's Asian BBQ special is also a winner. However, make sure to bring your patience; despite the layout of the restaurant's outdoor space – an arm's length from the sidewalk and the equivalent of a bouncer's width from the Maybachs crawling down Collins – Kung Fu Kitchen is frequently full by 10pm or so. If so, slide over to the Catalina's other canteen, Maxine's.

Miss Yip Café (bottom)

*1661 Meridian Avenue
(Lincoln Ln N), South Beach
Tel: 305 534 5488
www.missyipchinesecafe.com
Open: daily, noon–11pm
(midnight Fri/Sat)*

The titular Miss Yip isn't fictional. The proprietress is Jennie Yip, a New-York-born dynamo who has professional ties to Miami's Townhouse Hotel and the Wave department store in Bangkok. She also opened the Blue Door at the Delano, and created the food and beverage programs at a number of influential hotels and restaurants in New York City, so she clearly has a practiced eye and a developed set of taste buds. Miss Yip offers the best selection of Chinese food in the area, and it's frequently packed, the air filled with cheerful chat-

snack…

ter and the sound of clanging woks and sizzling broccoli. This is not an especially hip venue – see the faux apothecary jars filled with beer bottles and candy – but the dim sum, Cantonese and Sichuan staples attract a diverse crowd that regularly returns. The dark red leather sofas complemented by the flowery wallpaper and smudged mirrors give the interior that ever so shabby-chic feel. Afterwards, pay your respects to Miss Yip's artistic and alcohol-shaped sensibilities with a trip to her trendy Buck 15 bar upstairs (enter via the alley around the block).

Morgan's *(top)*
28 NE 29th Street (N Miami Ave), Downtown
Tel: 305 573 9678
www.themorgansrestaurant.com
Open: 11am–10pm (11pm Fri/Sat), 8am–5pm Sun. Closed Mondays.

Morgan's is a local establishment that serves familiar American comfort food with a tweak or two in a likeably homey setting. The likes of sturdy meatloaf, skirt steak salad, and 'naked' chicken pot pie amiably allow steamed coconut mussels, hummus plate and Moroccan stew onto the menu. The dining spaces are all of different characters and create interest – there's a table or two in the tiny garden, and families fill a casual outdoor porch-type setting anchored by several long, (faux) weathered wooden tables. There's also a first-level room in spare white, and another two small but stylish ones upstairs (the only section that reminds you you're in the Design District). All in all, if you're already here in the neighbourhood

looking for artsy accoutrements to take home, the reasonably priced Morgan's is assuredly worth a look (besides, there isn't an eatery of this calibre for blocks and blocks).

News Café *(left)*
800 Ocean Drive (8th St), South Beach
Tel: 305 538 6397
www.newscafe.com
Open: daily, 24 hours

If anything can be termed an 'original' on South Beach, it's this ultra-chill outdoor patio that opened in '88 (before the Miami renaissance). At the start, it was a simple bookstore and newsstand (still here), and the European café vibe that was generated with the addition of a few umbrella-shaded tables and a short menu of staples, enveloped by some jazz and classical music piped in at conversation-volume. News Café has expanded to include an extremely pleasant (and active) courtyard overshadowed by decorative globes and sea-grape trees whose twisted arms are so densely packed that they block out the sun. The menu is voluminous, so if you enjoy the experience of resting and gorging lazily among those who have no sense of time, there's no need to opt for the same meal twice.

Pasha's *(right)*
900 Lincoln Road (Jefferson Ave), Miami Beach
Tel: 305 673 3919
www.pashas.com
Open: daily, 8am–midnight (1am Fri/Sat)

snack...

There's only one reason a simple Mediterranean joint should look as cleanly designed as this one does. It owes its IKEA-ready face to its prime location on the corner of Lincoln Road, every bit as sparkly as its competitor neighbours. Pasha's falafel dishes are tops (the balls are chewily spongy and greaseless), the kebab platters (beef, chicken, lamb, veggie or salmon) are filling, and some say the rice that accompanies many items on the menu is the best in the world. Everything on the menu is inviting and remarkably bright-tasting, though ignore the grilled vegetable side orders as they're the only things at Pasha's that are overpriced. Try a veggie wrap or a ground chicken pide (the Turkish version of pizza) chased by a just-blended tangerine or melon juice. Needless to say, vegetarians will fall in love with the place and never want to dine anywhere else. Indeed, Pasha's is the healthiest snackery around, an oasis among the diet-busting ice-cream parlours and overstuffed plate purveyors on the strip.

Patagonia *(top)*
244 Miracle Mile (Ponce De Leon Blvd), Coral Gables
Tel: 305 640 8376
www.patagoniausa.net
Open: daily, 8am–9pm

Amongst the chi-chi boutiques and somewhat formal eateries on the Mile, Patagonia stands out for its casual attitude toward hospitality. That's not to say the courteous workers here aren't serious about providing an enjoyable break from the wealth on display outside. The Argentinean specialities here will more than meet your needs – if you're seeking a hearty lunch, tuck into the tender grilled meats available at the rear; for a mid-morning pick-me-up, opt for a cappuccino and a croissant (the traditional *alfajores* incorporate dulce du leche, as do several of the delicious pastries on offer). Set off from the order counters and surrounded by wine bottles, the handful of red tables give the illusion that they're in a venue one or two levels higher on the evolutionary scale. Patagonia is a rare affordable choice in the Gables that will leave you feeling satisfied and not financially cheated. If you're in the mood to lounge a bit, there's a sizeable selection of South American wines, but even these are reasonably priced.

Pelican Café *(bottom)*
826 Ocean Drive (8th St),
South Beach
Tel: 305 673 1000
www.pelicanhotel.com
Open: daily, 7.30am–12.30am

The Pelican Café is looking for a slightly more sophisticated class of clientele than those who are won over by the army of Ocean Drive hawkers, touting restaurants that cook a few dishes and leave them out on display to fester all day. And perhaps owing to the smart and somewhat esoteric attached hotel, your eating space is unusually attractive. On cloudy days or in the early evening, try the cosy interior with green and red leather booths. But most often the sidewalk option is best, with bright white chairs and thin black marble-topped tables nestling among the pleasantly overgrown greenery. The

menu is Italian-centric and vegetarian-friendly, with high-quality pastas, salads and sandwiches. If the Pelican is full, then try the News Café (south) or Cardozo (north) along the Drive.

- - -

La Sandwicherie *(left)*
229 14th Street (Collins Ct),
South Beach
Tel: 305 532 8934
www.lasandwicherie.com
Open: daily, 8am–5am

Miami Beach, so focused on the twin pleasures of lounging and laziness, is somehow not strong on the portable meal, save for the few fast food options strung along Collins and Washington. The best chance for a decent beach picnic meal is La Sandwicherie, which has crammed baguettes full of turkey and Camembert since 1988. It's worth paying attention to watch how fast the staffers can stuff these baguettes full of delicious ingredients: thirty-five seconds remains the record for a ham, turkey and salad baguette with extra French dressing and jalapenos. You can also decide to stay and sit at the bar, which serves no alcohol but makes up for it with smoothies and lip-smackingly good fruit or veggie juices. And since it's open until the drinking establishments bar the doors, La Sandwicherie is perfect for creatures who have the late-night munchies. Sandwiches are very well filled – there are eight possible toppings, plus mayo or vinaigrette – and can easily be shared.

- - -

Segafredo *(right)*
1040 Lincoln Road (Lenox),
South Beach

Tel: 305 673 0047
www.segafredo.it
Open: daily, 11am–1am (2am Fri/Sat)

Top Italian espresso producer Segafredo claims that 50 million of its drinks are downed each and every day. It's possible that one million of those could be generated in this Lincoln Road storefront – after all, Miamians need something to keep them fizzing with activity from dawn to the wee hours (and cocaine is oh-so 80s). At the non-caffeine end of the spectrum, one could either get stuck into the Martini list or do it European-style with a glass of red wine as you pass judgement on the outfits of passers-by (at Segafredo there are no two ways about it: you have to get stuck in and have an opinion on all fashion matters if you are to blend in properly). It's the kind of place where Latin men undo the bow at the back of the waitress's apron and then snigger, where peroxide blondes chain-smoke and talk about Gucci jumpers, and where you snack on salads, carpaccio and paninis at lunchtime or after work. However, don't get any ideas about arriving in the a.m. and expecting breakfast – this is a no-pastry zone. This is an Italian coffee bar on the widest catwalk in Miami, and should be approached accordingly.

- - -

Shake Shack *(bottom)*
1111 Lincoln Road (Alton Rd),
Miami Beach
Tel: 305 434 7787
www.shakeshack.com
Open: daily, 11.30am–1am

Floridians are passionate about their burgers, and Shake Shack's are the

snack...

subject of much debate in the venue's original New York home. Many citizens think they're the best in the city, while others are unimpressed. The propriety blend of meats ground up (courtesy of the master butchers at Pat La Frieda Meats) are reliably juicy and attractive, with their time on the grill leaving them with a touch of crispiness on the outside and a thin pink layer within – you'll never be faced with one of those sad, flat, grey-tinged patties. The fresh-off-Lincoln-Road clientele is attractive too, and patient – waiting times can stretch into double digits (it's fast food, but not that fast). The crinkle-cut fries and hotdogs are almost as worthy, but you should really splurge on a concrete (frozen custard spun up with a raft of ingredients); utterly addictive and yet too much not to share.

Tapas Y Tintos *(top)*
448 Española Way (Drexel),
South Beach
Tel: 305 538 8272
www.tapasytintos.com
Open: daily, noon–1am (2am Sat/Sun)

Tapas y Tintos is a Spanish tapas bar that's often filled with Iberian ex-pats longing for a taste of home. It rests on Española Way, which appears to be the closest thing to España on the island. Many of the tapas are commendable, although the *patatas bravas* usually elicits harsh words from diners. This place is always packed despite its reputation for poor service – wildly inconsistent at best, downright rude at worst – and is best for snacks and

early sangria sipping before heading off to a more serious dining location.

Tiramesu *(bottom)*
721 Lincoln Road
(Meridian Ave), Miami Beach
Tel: 305 532 4538
www.tiramesu.com
Open: daily, 11am–11pm
(midnight Fri/Sat)

Even the locals frequent Tiramesu, which is as Italian as the dessert it's named for (well, there's a limit as to how Mediterranean you can get in Florida). The relentlessly cheery restaurant – complete with screaming blue awnings and sunflowers on the tables – is looked upon as a consistently reliable choice among the more tourist-oriented options on the Road, and still able to attract a moderately chic audience. It's also one of the few eateries round these parts that cares enough about the end product to make its own bread and pasta. The menu holds 20 classic and regional dishes, including two vegan pastas, plus the requisite meat and fish preparations, crudos and antipasti, risottos and a meat-and-cheese board. Finally, if you are tempted to indulge in the creamy dessert after which this establishment is named, it is reportedly worth the investment.

snack...

The Van Dyke Café *(below)*

846 Lincoln Road
(Jefferson Ave), Miami Beach
Tel: 305 534 3600
www.thevandykecafe.com
Open: daily, 8am–1am (2am Sat/Sun)

A music lounge and café, the Van Dyke is seemingly popular with just about everyone, from weary shoppers to tourists to skateboarders. The building, created by August Geiger in 1924, towers above everything but the Sony headquarters and the Sun Trust Bank that lie on either end of Lincoln Road. For that reason – and for the red English phone box and the blanket of creeping ivy that covers the building – the Van Dyke Café cuts a dashing figure in comparison to the poured-concrete walls of most of the neighbouring buildings. The ground floor is dedicated to the café, offering burgers, salads, Middle Eastern mezes and pastas. The second level, formally christened 'Upstairs at the Van Dyke', features live music nightly from 9pm to 1am. While the Van Dyke name was traditionally associated with jazz – and still puts on a regular Thursday jazz series – Upstairs now spotlights a variety of genres, including funk, Latin/Cuban and R&B (check out the calendar on its website for specifics).

11th Street Diner

snack...

party...

You've checked in, tanned, wined and dined. Now what? Welcome to the fashion show that never sleeps, to the city where you can drink Martinis and mojitos shoulder-to-shoulder with designer-clad models, movie stars and self-acclaimed SoBe superstars – provided the doorman lets you slip past the notoriously taut velvet ropes, that is. The Miami party scene is a force to be reckoned with, possessing the power to make or break your reputation for as long as you're on location.

Unfortunately, if you're visiting now, you've missed Miami's heyday. A decade ago legendary clubs such as Liquid, Warsaw and Crobar defined late-night dancing and debauchery in Miami, sponsoring jaw-dropping parties until sunrise every morning. Warsaw was particularly raucous – one never knew if the club would be strewn in foliage from top to bottom for a woodland-themed party or feature a cadre of strippers with overactive imaginations and flexible limbs. Crobar's Backdoor Bamby party was a weekly gay/straight night where all lines became increasingly blurred as the night evolved. Even as recently as five years ago, Prive and Rumi, among others, offered many alternatives for the dancing dipsomaniac. Regrettably, the worldwide recession changed much of that. Miami has fared better than some other American cities (i.e. Las Vegas), but even with $20 cover charges, party spaces need a boatload of dependable revellers just to stay afloat. Now, as then, the landscape changes continually; what is at its peak today may be a distant memory come next Thursday in this fabulously fickle Floridian city. Many of the current hip venues are owned by the Opium Group, which eschews the community aspect of clubbing and tries to maintain an elitist feeling with obnoxious door policies.

On the weekend the top clubs implore you to 'dress to impress'. What this means is anyone's guess, and requirements ease somewhat if you reserve a table or have your name on the guest list. Men – don anything with a designer label, make sure your gold chain is on display between suitably swirly chest hair and stuff a sock down your drawers (most places have a 'no trainers' rule, too). As for attitude, pretend they should be paying you to come in and you'll be slapped on the back and ushered into the first circle. Failure to do so will have you tossed onto the pavement with the rest of the night's riff-raff. Girls have it rather easier than men – stick some rollers in your hair, lather on the lipgloss and wear as little as you possibly can without being arrested for public indecency. With any luck you won't have to pay for a single drink. If you happen to be looking for that long-lost sugar daddy, there

is a strong possibility that he is sitting in one of Miami's lounges, doling out shots from his $400 bottle of vodka, and waiting for you to come and sit on his knee.

In South Beach the party scene often revolves around VIP lounges and the astronomic charges for the privilege of consuming a $40 bottle of alcohol in a barely-private cordoned-off block. Door policies range from easy to ridiculous, and everywhere you go, cash is king – the more green you are prepared to drop, the more cachet you generate.

However, don't feel you have to embrace the foolishness and jump through hoops to fully experience what Miami has to offer. And brush aside illusions that you're just too important to enlist the services of your hotel concierge; he/she and his/her corps of contacts could be your ticket to relative celebrity for one brief, six-hour window. The Catalina has a particularly good one that prints up a nightly menu of possibilities.

How to manage your drinking & dancing days and dollars...

You're here on vacation, so every night is pretty much an opportunity for fresh revelry. What to do? Here's where Hg2 gives you a play-by-play map for a week on your social calendar – where to go on each evening to maximize your mood, chill you out and/or find someone to cut loose with (note: several venues mentioned below are not included in the Party or Drink chapters; you should be able to find them without too much trouble. If in doubt, ask another partygoer or your hotel concierge).

Monday: there's only one certainty, and that's Tantra, which has owned Monday nights with its internationally-sourced house mixes for as long as anyone's liquor-addled brain can remember. The only other credible pretender is B.E.D., where the long-standing Secret Society party (now Hush Mondays) serves as a somewhat more laid-back alternative.

Tuesday: perhaps the most difficult night to schedule, Tuesday should be reserved for less participatory pursuits. It's probably a fine time to check out Van Dyke Café; you can expect to be surprised, as the unsettled Tuesday rotating plan might consist of an acoustic guitarist, a quartet playing jazz standards, a pop/jazz chanteuse or Argentinean folk artists. Oh, screw it – it's great fun to be part of Louis' lively Viva La Revolución, as the fog and strobes are calibrated to make you think it's the weekend already.

Wednesday: time to decide – up- or down market tonight? For the latter, take a spin over to Purdy Lounge for electro/indie hits and some billiards, or to Lincoln Lane for 'Old Skool' at Buck 15. Alternatively, put on your best duds and a serious game face (for the bouncers) to blend in under the violet sky at LIV.

Thursday: the recently redone Wall lounge at the W Hotel can provide some diversion, but it's certainly not as hot as the chilly neon blue and lavender glow of the Bleau Bar in the Fontainebleau's lobby (once tired of standing around in public, walk several steps to Arkadia a more intimate lounge space than the adjacent LIV). Anyone who blew off the Monday and settled for a sushi dinner instead could opt for B.E.D. or Tantra tonight. You could, of course, use this opportunity to take off and gear up in anticipation of a weekend of fizz and flash, but … you won't.

Friday: you're really spoiled for choice, as the weekend is now fully underway and venues both mega and minor break out the heavy artillery. Hip-hop features prominently, as Mansion, Cameo and Mokai all spotlight crunkier sounds. House or open format is on order everywhere else, whipping patrons into a state of positive high energy at Mynt and Set. According to management, there's Dirty Sexy Rock 'N' Roll at Rok Bar (but for us, the hugely overpriced bottles served tableside present more as Douchey Faux Sexy Poser). The Florida Room (at the Delano) and Sky Bar (at the Shore Club) are the only other real selections besides Louis, whose DJs spin indie/electro/hip-hop at the seemingly accurately named Misfit Fridays. For those who have already ruled out a Saturday night in Downtown, go to Mekka, recommended for its four themed areas and the most welcoming club environment in greater Miami.

Saturday: the sixth day of the week is slightly less hectic than one would expect, and the best options involve you leaving the South Beach traffic jam altogether (a serious buzzkill awaits for anyone driving down Washington, Collins or Ocean between 11pm and 4am). For the ultimate in European club experiences, park yourself in Downtown, where, depending on your stamina, the newly renovated Space or Nocturnal (or both?) will speak to you in booming, flashing Morse code. If you want to break it up a bit, pop into Discotekka at Mekka, the room's gay night. If you must stay on the beach, try your luck with the performers at Jazid or take in Forbidden City, the Asian burlesque show at Kung Fu Kitchen. Another alternative: the loud and crunchy soundtrack at Automatic Slim's, which never disappoints.

Sunday: if you choose, you can skip the Sunday morning hangover/brunch and keep working it at the Downtown spaces 'til early afternoon, or squeeze into Sun-Daze at Sky Bar. To combine the best of two worlds (catching bpms and pigging out), Nikki Beach's Amazing Sunday is the ticket. Late night, a sleek trend-setting crowd shows up at LIV's door at the Fontainebleau hoping for quick entry, sonic booms and stiff cocktails.

B.E.D. *(top)*

*929 Washington Avenue
(9th St), South Beach
Tel: 305 532 9070
www.bedmiami.com
Open: 11pm–5am. Closed Sundays.*

Along with Mynt and Tantra, B.E.D. attracts Miami's elite. The letters are apparently an abbreviation for Beverage, Entertainment and Dining, but also signify the prevailing theme here. The room is full of enormous beds (capacity, 10) and heaped with mountains of cushions to lounge on. B.E.D. serves a sumptuous, French-style dinner with hints of Brazilian cuisine in two sittings; the 'first lay' begins at 8pm, the idea being to eat as the Romans did back in the day when South Beach was still a swamp. B.E.D. wakes up at 11pm when the doors open to non-diners. Every night is controlled by a different DJ and set-up, for instance Monday's 'Secret Society' hip-hop night is the club's busiest night and also the hardest to get into. Come for dinner and linger, or enter at the tail-end of the last seating to avoid paying the cover. There is a 'fashionably hip and chic' dress code, so save the Green Flash trainers for Nocturnal at the weekend.

LIV *(middle)*

*The Fontainebleau, 4441
Collins Avenue, Mid-Beach
Tel: 305 674 4680
www.livnightclub.com
Open: 11pm–5am Wed, Fri–Sun*

LIV encapsulates entertainment, both expensive and expansive. As a breed of club for the twenty-first century, it's all these things and more, but perhaps due to its home at the Fontainebleau it is a touch too glossy and corporate. That's not to say that a certain level of raucousness can't be attained here. The premises are indeed stunning, taken in as you descend the branched arcing staircase like the royalty you imagine you are (remember to bow down to the DJ in his turntable fortress in the centre). The cavernous space is capped with a big top/planetarium dome ceiling radiating light, which supports the killer metal spider that holds the high-tech lighting scheme and random glitter globes. Open cubes frame visiting VIPs high above the masses, who move absentmindedly to the succession of Ozzy remixes, pop and hip-hop that emanates from the ridiculously complex sound system.

Louis *(bottom)*

*Gansevoort Miami Beach, 2377
Collins Avenue (24th St), South Beach
Tel: 305 531 4600
www.louismiami.com
Open: 11pm–5am Tues, Thurs–Sat*

A self-described 'royal Parisian palace on a happy acid trip', Louis takes as its inspiration the period before the French Revolution, when a certain bewigged queen and spouse of Louis the Fourteenth shouted, "Let them eat cake!" There are no pastries here, but plenty of baked, minimally polished frat boys trying too hard to catch the eye of that passing spangly halter dress. The masses (a tad more age-diverse than in other dance halls) shake their thangs to electro-pop remixes in an admittedly cool room in which velvet fleur-de-

MANSION TONIGHT

lys wallpaper, powdered wigs in glass cases, antique furniture and stripes and leopard prints all compete for the attention of the non-dancers. Occasionally, a little person in Napolean-inspired attire will dance on the bar and shoot out cold smoke from a high pressure canister to make sure everyone is still wide awake. Louis provides for quite a fun evening, and doesn't leave you with the feeling – all too common in the Magic City – that your cash would've been better spent elsewhere.

Mansion *(top)*
1235 Washington Avenue (12th St),
South Beach
Tel: 305 532 1525
www.mansionmiami.com
Open: 11pm–5am Tues, Thurs–Sat

Mansion is very Miami, endeavouring to pack 2,500 Barbies and Kens into six VIP areas and five dance rooms, charging $20 entry and $10 a drink, cranking up the house music and counting all the cash when the cleaning crew shows up. Housed in what was originally the French Casino when it opened in 1936, Mansion spans over 40,000-square-feet and is adorned with period chandeliers, fireplaces, Venetian mirrors, exposed brick, creeping ivy, keystone arches and six projection screens. DJs and occasional special guests predominate, while hip-hop takes over on Fridays. If you can't get in, head across the street to Automatic Slims – a much more democratic party palace.

Mekka *(middle)*
950 NE 2nd Avenue
(NE 10th St), Downtown

Tel: 305 371 3773
www.mekkamiami.com
Open: 11pm–noon Fri–Sun

Anyone who's a bit jaded with the whole party scene may very well want to check out Mekka – it's four (or five) clubs in one, each with an individual mood and soundtrack. Mekka occupies the central space (with the largest bar area), observed from above by the DJs spinning atop a gigantic boom box. Goddess is slinky and sultry, and Forbidden vaguely brings to mind an unnerving combination of bondage and the Far East. Perhaps the most fun can be had at Vibe, light and funky and with a democratic feel that allows the bouncing patrons to share the stage with the turntable doctor. Gay rave Discotekka is reserved for Saturdays. The original developers of Mekka imagined that they would control one large space, leasing out the smaller subsidiary rooms to four separate entities, but the plan was scrapped in favour of developing the outer rooms themselves – and Mekka flourishes as a result. The parking situation is a bit rough, so if you can, arrive in something discreet, transportation-wise.

Mynt Lounge *(bottom)*
1921 Collins Avenue (20th St),
South Beach
Tel: 305 532 0727
www.myntlounge.com
Open: 11pm–5am Wed–Sat

Followers of the MB social scene have no idea why Mynt is still as popular as it is; its 15 minutes of fame should have expired long ago. But if you want to see the most beautiful girls on South

Beach drink vodka in Russian proportions and convince Miami's insanely wealthy men to pick up the bill, then go. Mynt holds conflicting ideals; it claims 'the customer is the star' and 'elegance, chic and a winning smile' are the minimum requirements for entry, but don't believe it. Instead, believe you are a superstar and getting in will go smoothly; otherwise you will be relegated to the ranks of the autograph hunters outside. Once inside, you'll find three aisles of cream sofas laden with golddiggers and celebrities. If the booming house and trance music is all a bit much, then go next door to Rok Bar.

....

Nikki Beach *(bottom)*
1 Ocean Drive (1st St),
South Beach
Tel: 305 538 1111
www.nikkibeach.com
Open: daily, 7am–5am

Located on the southern end of South Beach, Nikki Beach was once dubbed the sexiest place on Earth. Now it's a little more mature, but it's still the sexiest place in Miami. Not just a beach club, but a luxury spa and restaurant, you could spend an entire day and the most part of the evening lounging here. Sexy Saturday is Nikki Beach's trademark, luring people off the beaches to laze on massive square platforms padded with white pillows, on hammocks and in private love dens on stilts while hypnotic house beats are pumped out by the DJ. For a chilled morning after, drag yourself out of bed for the amazing Sunday event, featuring a brunch buffet with a Belgian waffle station and a smoked salmon carver – known as the best in the area.

Nocturnal *(left)*
50 NE 11th Street (NE 1st Ave),
Downtown
Tel: 305 576 6996
www.nocturnalmiami.com
Open: 11pm–11am Fri, Sat

A 20,000-square-foot state-of-the-art superclub spread over three floors, Nocturnal is the underappreciated sibling to Space's Prom Queen next door. The first level houses a main dance floor with three bars and a café, while the balcony-bordered second floor is where the VIPs are bunkered, flanked by two rooms in which to conduct those intimate conversations that inevitably take place in strobe-filled superclubs (a glassed-in lounge and a smaller space with tables). Floor number three is home to the rooftop patio (with waterfall), where clubbers can bounce while the sun ascends. The experience is boosted by the most elaborate sound and lighting system known to man.

....

Score *(right)*
727 Lincoln Road
(Washington Ave), South Beach
Tel: 305 535 1111
www.scorebar.net
Open: daily, 3pm–5am

The Miami area doesn't really have a 'gaybourhood', just individual, scattered locations. If it did, Score could serve as its epicentre; it's well-located, loud and lively. One can sit outside and watch the beautiful people shop on Lincoln Road, or enter the chic, mirrored front bar and discuss current events with handsome Latinos and muscle boys. The main space boasts high-tech lighting and 'the biggest disco ball in

party...

the country', while upstairs comes with a separate sound system and functions as a more intimate setting (if your idea of intimate includes a stripper pole). Score is hetero-friendly, but the vast majority of the clients are there to meet someone of the same sex. It remains one of the bastions of the gay community on South Beach, with a black-clad male staff that's requisitely cool (in demeanour) and smoulderingly hot (in appearance).

Skyline *(top)*
645 Washington Avenue (6th St), South Beach
Tel: 786 333 8441
www.skylinemia.com
Open: 10pm–5am Thurs–Sat

For those whose Mile High Club ambitions have been thus far frustrated, the (literally) jet-conscious Skyline is for you. Once you enter through the vacuum-lock emergency door, proceed along the lighted walkways to the bar – outfitted with replica twin turbo-propeller engines so you don't miss it – and ask the 'flight crew' for something to drink (these are probably made with some of those snack-size liquor bottles – they're tiny and strong, served in flimsy plastic). Lazy passengers can sit in actual aircraft seats around a (non-foldaway) Formica table, while VIPs get a larger setup with a 'personal stewardess'. Tired of sitting? Dance before the nose of a dissembled commercial jet, from which, naturally, the DJ directs the mood of patrons and shoots lasers.

Space *(left)*
34 NE 11th Street (N Miami Ave), Downtown
Tel: 305 375 0001
www.clubspace.com
Open: 10pm–10am Sat (check website schedule for additional days/events)

Downtown is the only part of Miami that issues 24-hour liquor licenses, and at the weekends Space is its answer to Ibiza, attracting the Royal Family of DJs. Deep Dish, Danny Tenaglia, Tiësto and Paul van Dyk are regulars, while Paul Oakenfold, Junior Vasquez and Sasha and Digweed have all made guest appearances at what has been voted the top club in the USA (courtesy of DJ Mag). Radamas (hailing from the Bronx), Maurizio + Danyelino (Italy) and Boris (St. Petersburg) make up the core of internationally-flavoured resident spinners. Meanwhile, owner (and occasional DJ) Louis Puig has thirty years under his shiny studded belt as a jack-of-all-trades of the nightclub experience (bartender, promoter, builder, designer, sound and light guy), so you know the former warehouse has been crammed to the brim with intricate lighting and sound systems (all upgraded in 2010). The main dance floor is surrounded by bars, and there's a rooftop terrace for movers who don't have to retire to their vampire coffins when the sun rises.

Tantra *(right)*
1445 Pennsylvania Avenue (Espanola Way), South Beach
Tel: 305 672 4765
www.tantra-restaurant.com

FIRST CLASS III

SKYL

party...

Open: 7pm–2am Thurs (3am Wed, 5am Mon, Fri and Sat, hours variable Sun and Tues)

In dog years, Tantra may be ancient, and even compared to the normal Miami nightspot lifecycle it's 'mature'. However, Tantra shows no signs of letting up its death grip on the club scene – its Monday night parties have been etched into the socialite calendar for more than a decade. It may have something to do with the setting, which is punctuated with furniture and art pieces gathered from the owner's travels in Asia, and results in an undoubtedly sensual vibe. You may wish to dine here (on tempting but expensive aphrodisiacal cuisine), but the raison d'être is imbibing and dancing on the tables. The crowd is ridiculously good looking; models of all ethnicities drink as many cocktails as possible without falling down on the grass-covered area next to the bar, while ex-frat boys gone wild ape the stars of MTV's Jersey Shore (who popped up here regularly on the show). Fist pump!

Twist *(bottom)*
1057 Washington Avenue (11th St), South Beach
Tel: 305 538 9478
www.twistsobe.com
Open: daily, 1pm–5am

Do not be alarmed if you see men adjusting their dresses outside – it's just a regular Wednesday night. Originally one small, dark bar, Twist is now the biggest gay club in Miami, boasting six separate spaces over two levels (each of which looks like it came out of a separate nightclub) plus a bungalow bar and muscled male dancers who perform seven nights a week. With a reduced number of venues to choose from, Twist has become the gay flag bearer on the Beach. Twist offers two-for-one drinks in the dark-lit entry bar from 1 until 9pm – one of the most generous happy hour deals around. Twist plays a mixture of house, hip-hop and pop remixes, in the same style as most nightclubs and lounges on South Beach. The atmosphere is always very friendly, and the male clientele makes up a varied group of twinks, older gents and sluts-in-training. Also it is increasingly common for groups of party girls to end up at Twist, much to the dismay of the gentlemen, with dollar bills they're aching to part with. Once the tableau gets tired, the 11th Street Diner is next door for some after-Twist munchies.

LIVE MUSIC

Residents don't have much of a taste for it, and visitors don't have the attention span to watch a band play hour-long sets. That must explain why rooms with live music are hard to find. Jazid, the Van Dyke Café (Upstairs) and Transit Lounge (described in the Drink and Snack sections) are always good for some interesting performances. Bayfront Park and the Fillmore Miami Beach are additional options for the more popular travelling bands and singer/songwriters (see Culture).

CASINOS

Magic City Casino
450 NW 37th Avenue (NW 4th Terrace), Downtown
Tel: 305 649 3000
www.flaglerdogs.com
Open: daily, 10am–4am

A Las Vegas-style casino within a short ride of Downtown and Miami Beach, Magic City has just about everything to make a gambler's palms start sweating. Besides 800 slot machines, the hopeful throw cash away on poker (No Limit Texas Hold 'em from noon to 4am) and dog racing simulcasts (from a Naples, Florida track). Those trying to stem

their losses can cool down in the restaurant or two bars. The full roster of concerts and events put on here can be found on the casino's website.

STRIP CLUBS

Club Madonna

1527 Washington Avenue (16th St), South Beach
Tel: 305 534 2000
www.clubmadonna.com
Open: daily, 6pm–6am

Club Madonna is the only serious stripping joint on South Beach. Look for a large window with a woman sitting on a throne inside and a stretch limo with strippers painted onto it. Madonna's has one main room with a central stage and two additional mini stages, with seating areas around them. The girls are not renowned for their beauty, but given the distinct lack of options on South Beach, Madonna's is popular, mainly with tourists. Be sure to look at your credit card bill at the end of the evening, and be warned that hiring the VIP room is not advised.

Dean's Gold
2355 NE 163rd Street (Biscayne Blvd), North Miami
Tel: 305 956 5726 www.deansgold.com
Open: 3pm (6pm Sat, 8pm Sun)–6am daily

It's a 15-minute drive from South Beach, but Dean's Gold is widely regarded as the finest gentleman's club in the area, catering for both men and women, gay and straight. If you want to see men, turn left at the entrance, for women turn right. Of the three adult entertainment establishments listed in this guide, the girls that work at Dean's Gold are the closest to what would be described as erotic dancers. Guests are escorted to sofas with a view of the stage, although there is seating around the stage from which men attach money to girls.

Tootsies Cabaret
150 NW 183rd Street
(NW 2nd Ave), North Miami
Tel: 305 651 5822
www.tootsiescabaret.com
Open: daily, noon–5am

Classy is not a word that springs to mind when you're having your passport photocopied at the door. Tootsies is the most graphic strip club in Miami. It looks like a fast-food joint, serving beer and tacos, but the dozens of naked girls walking around the stage remind customers why they paid $5 to get in. There is nothing left to the imagination at Tootsies; the room is well-lit and the dancers, who weren't really wearing much to begin with anyway, get down from the stage after their acts and give clients on the front row a close-up in return for one-dollar bills. Tootsies is not so much seedy, it's just honest. The wheel of friction competition, when the evening's host spins a giant wheel to decide which lucky customer wins the 'jackpot', is the undisputed highlight.

Hg2 in interview with Robbie Rivera…

If anyone knows anything about Miami's nightlife, it's dance floor don Robbie Rivera. Born in Puerto Rico, the superstar DJ has scaled the charts to become one of the most prolific house music producers in the world – particularly in Miami, where his annual Juicy Beach parties at Nikki Beach during the Winter Music Conference have thousands of revelers first-pumping in the air like they just don't care. Hg2 managed to steal Robbie away from the turntables long enough to quiz him about his hedonistic home-away-from-home.

What marks you out from the dance floor crowd?
Robbie Rivera: I stand out because I am unique, diverse and innovative. And modest. [laughs]

How would you describe Miami?
Robbie Rivera: That's easy! Miami is sunny, exciting, exhilarating, cutting-edge, fun, sexy. The weather is so that you can always do many outdoor activities during the day and at night.

In Miami, what's your favourite...

Hotel?

Robbie Rivera: I never stay in hotels in Miami as I live there! However, if I had to recommend one, I would stay at The Setai because it is sophisticated and luxurious.

Bar?

Robbie Rivera: Bardot Miami in midtown, and also Bougainvillea's in South Miami. Both of these venues have live bands that play a wide array of music from rock to reggae. It's a nice change to all of the usual bangin' club music type of venues.

Restaurant?

Robbie Rivera: Houston's in Coral Gables and Puntino in Key Biscayne. Houston's has outstanding cuisine, most notably their great steaks, ribs and seafood. They have been around for a long time and there is always a line to get in for dining. They have a great bar, as well. I love the atmosphere in the bar. Puntino is Key Biscayne quite simply serves amazing, delicious Italian cuisine.

Club?

Robbie Rivera: Mynt Lounge. I like this club because the average age of the patron is around 30-years-old, so it is more of an adult vibe. Also, the soundsystem and lighting systems are amazing and state-of-the-art. The owner is a nice guy, as well.

Shop?

Robbie Rivera: Neiman Marcus! I go here because I love buying nice clothes. [laughs] I admit it. I travel a lot, so I like to buy good-quality clothing because I put my clothes – and shoes, and luggage, etc. – through a lot.

Spa?

Robbie Rivera: I have no idea! I've never been to one. But, I hear Canyon Ranch is awesome.

Beach?

Robbie Rivera: Key Biscayne beach in front of my condo if terrific! If you want to see lots of surgically enhanced ladies, though, I suggest Miami Beach between 1st and 10th Streets...but I haven't been there in a while. [laughs]

Landmark?

Robbie Rivera: Vizcaya Mansion. This is a landmark in Miami. It's a really beautiful mansion facing the water. You have to go there!

What's next for you?

Robbie Rivera: I'm finishing my new studio album and my North American tour...then it's Juicy Beach 2011 in Miami...and onward to Europe [to play] the big summer festivals and the superclubs in Ibiza, Spain, and beyond. I am also planning my fall-winter 2011-2012 shows, so I am always working far in advance. What people sometimes might not realize if they're not working in the dance music industry is that there's a lot of work that goes into the shows. It's not just the show itself; it's all of the planning and production and negotiating and creation that goes on behind-the-scenes before the actual show happens. And then you're on to booking the next shows. It never really ends and I like it that way.

party...

culture...

Miami is not naturally gifted, culturally speaking. Yes, there are several noteworthy intellectual venues, but nothing on the scale of London or Boston, and the 'formal' arts community that formed in the latter years of the twentieth century was developed only with a considerable amount of effort.

Downtown has two notable sites among the ultra-touristy attractions. First, and most visibly obvious, is the Arsht Center, a behemoth buoyed by glass and light. It's a recent addition to the cityscape, where the orchestral concert, opera or dance performance is only one element of the experience. Hidden away southwest of the city is the European-style early 1900s manor Vizcaya, which is far from being another stuffy museum. It comes alive in the room descriptions and in the extensive gardens in which you are free to roam about in until closing.

Further out, Coral Gables is one of the U.S.'s first planned communities and immediately distinguishable because of its Spanish-influenced architecture. It is worth a morning out to walk around the district, but if you're pressed for time just get to the Venetian pool or the Biltmore Hotel.

The apparently cultureless district of South Beach is nowhere near as artistically barren as it first appears. You can see it, first and foremost, in its bones; Miami is the largest preserved historic district in the country for its 800-odd Art Deco buildings constructed in the 1930s and 1940s. On a more serious note, the large Jewish communities here have contributed to the establishment of the Ziff Jewish Museum and the Holocaust memorial (and its striking Sculpture of Love and Anguish), which manage to be both disturbing and inspiring.

Some of Florida's top art centres are here as well, including Britto Central (the base of Brazilian artist Romero Britto) and the Bass Museum of Art. In fact, in a confluence of creativity and the city's ever-evident celebrity culture, a notable art festival was born. Since 2002, Art Basel Miami Beach (an offshoot of the larger, more respected annual event in Switzerland) has attracted up-and-coming sculptors, performance and video artists and paint-splatterers, as well as the moneyed elite which hopes to catch lightning in a bottle by snapping up the next best pieces for long-term lucrative investments.

Arsht Center

Many might associate Miami with its reputation as the home of all manner of in-your-face public (almost) nudity. To temper your excitement with a little knowledge, stop by the World Erotic Arts Museum (conveniently located among the tattoo parlours on Washington Avenue) and remind yourself that nakedness and sensuality have been a part of intellectual and sociological discussions since, like, always.

In spite of the worthy artistic and historic locations mentioned below, Miami is essentially a party city, and is not generally renowned for its cultural options. So pop along to a gallery, wander around Vizcaya or absorb some history – it'll go some way to convincing you your time hasn't been wasted entirely on frivolous pursuits.

Adrienne Arsht Center *(top)*
for the Performing Arts

1300 Biscayne Boulevard (NE 13th St),
Downtown
Tel: 305 949 6722
www.arshtcenter.org

It doesn't seem as though any of the $470 million that went into this project was wasted. It's all evident in the details and in the larger-than-life presence of this lovely complex, which appears as a well-lit off-kilter stack of books or a well-behaved Frank Gehry construction as you approach from I-395. The main components are a ballet/opera house, a concert hall, a smaller theatre and an open plaza, but the Arsht Center also contains more than a few public art pieces and another winning Barton G.-backed restaurant. Cultured residents and visitors may be treated to a performance by the New World Symphony, the Miami City Ballet or a touring Broadway show on any given night, and the whole plot was developed to serve as a destination for an entire evening.

Art Basel

Tel: 305 674 1292
www.artbaselmiamibeach.com

This annual festival, which lasts several days in early December and is arguably the most prestigious art show on the continent, has been instrumental in solidifying Miami's 'hot destination' reputation. Artworks on show – including large paintings, drawings and sculptures, as well as a growing contingent of video art, photography and installations – are the products of 2,000 artists from 250 top galleries across 29 countries. Each and every one is here to be viewed, buzzed about and sold. The number of gallery shows, film screenings and special events grows every season; past programmes have included an 'interactive food installation' and a site-specific mini-exhibition on an island in the bay that could only be visited via motorboat.

 Art Center South Florida
800 Lincoln Road (Meridian Ave),
South Beach
Tel: 305 674 8278
www.artcentersf.org
Open: daily, 11am–10pm (11pm Fri/Sat)

Make time to pop into this art centre at least one of the scores of times you'll likely be treading Lincoln Road. It's a non-profit organisation divided up into small, subsidised studio exhibitions by up-and-coming artists. Some of Miami's brightest young things work here, and since this isn't a fancy name, gallery prices are kept low. Visitors can often enter the studios and watch the artists work.

Art Deco *(bottom)*

Just take your head out of this guide and look up - you'll stumble upon grand Art Deco buildings (in various states of being) at every turn. In short, the style emerged as part of Paris' *Expostion Internationale des Arts Decoratifs et Industriels Modernes* in 1925. You can recognise the style (in both its Skyscraper and Streamline Moderne versions) by looking for porthole

windows, terrazzo floors, a sense of symmetry, stepped roofs, neon signage and lots of curves. L. Murray Dixon and Henry Hohauser, two of the architects working down here in that era, are significantly responsible for the feel of the Miami Beach structural landscape. Say a little prayer to honour the two people (Barbara Capitman and Leonard Horowitz) who are responsible for much of what you encounter here; that is, that it is still here. Ms. Capitman's efforts led to the establishment, in 1979, of the Miami Beach Architectural Historic District (or Art Deco District) and its inclusion on the National Register of Historic Places, which protects the buildings and, in most cases, prevents their demolition. According to author Gerald Posner, Mr. Horowitz convinced Ms. Capitman that the white and beige paint jobs accented with dark colours were depressing; she allowed him to apply the pastel palette of faded lime, violet, sky blue, rose and coral that gives today's South Beach so much of its character. If you're interested in learning more, a stop at the Miami Design Preservation League at 1001 Ocean Drive (www.mdpl.org) for some brochures or a tour is essential.

Bass Art Museum
2100 Collins Avenue (22nd St), South Beach
Tel: 305 673 7530
www.bassmuseum.org
Open: noon–5pm. Closed Mon/Tue.

The Bass was founded in 1963 when the City of Miami Beach accepted the gift of the art collection of John and Johanna Bass, now the epicentre of South Beach's art scene. The museum occupies what was originally the Miami Beach Public Library, which was designed in 1930 by Russell Pancoast, grandson of Miami Beach pioneer John A. Collins. The collection includes European masters, 18th-century English portraits, Chinese art and Flemish tapestries. The museum regularly exhibits several different travelling collections at the same time.

Bay of Pigs Museum *(top)*
1821 SW 9th Street (SW 18th Ave), Little Havana
Tel: 305 649 4719
Open: 9am–5pm. Closed Sun. Free.

The Bay of Pigs Museum tells the story of how Cuban exiles in Miami were trained by the CIA for a top secret mission to invade Cuba in April 1961. The 1,300-strong force was met by the Cuban army after landing in the Bay of Pigs (Bahia de Cochinos). Around 100 were killed, and the rest were captured and imprisoned. Singer Gloria Estefan's father was one of the men captured, and the survivors returned to the U.S. in 1962. Though interesting, the museum is tiny and almost all notes and captions are in Spanish, so don't build your day around a visit here.

Britto Central *(bottom)*
818 Lincoln Road (Meridian Ave), South Beach
Tel: 305 531 8821
www.britto.com
Open: daily, 10am–11pm (midnight Fri/Sat).

818

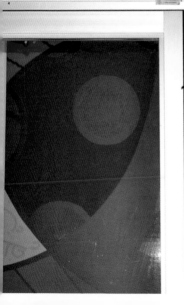

After spending his youth painting on scraps of cardboard and newspapers in Recife, Brazil, Romero Britto travelled to the United States in 1987 to pursue a career in graphic art. Since then his distinctive Pop Art style has been exhibited in over 100 galleries around the world, and has been plastered on bottles of Absolut and FIFA programs. The Miami gallery is Britto's headquarters.

Holocaust Memorial *(left)*
1933–1945 Meridian Avenue (19th St), South Beach
Tel: 305 538 1663
www.holocaustmmb.org
Open: daily, 9am–9pm. Free.

This powerful memorial is dedicated to the six million Jewish victims of the Holocaust. It was commissioned in 1985 and executed by sculptor Kenneth Treister, who described it as 'a large environmental sculpture… a series of outdoor spaces in which the visitor is led through a procession of visual, historical and emotional experiences with the hope that the totality of the visit will express, in some small way, the reality of the Holocaust. The dominant image is the large, 42-foot-tall bronze arm, The Sculpture of Love and Anguish, up which climb 130 bronze-cast human figures in various forms of anguish.

Rubell Family *(bottom)*
Collection
95 NW 29th Street (NW 1st Ave), Design District
Tel: 305 573 6090
www.rfc.museum
Open: Call for schedule.

The return of Miami to the upper echelons of American cities is due in part to Don and Mera Rubell and the opening of their museum in 1994 (they started amassing contemporary art when they got married). While respectable art institutions did already exist in the city, the RFC added both a tie to the 'serious' art world of New York and some associated glamour (some of the Rubells' money was inherited from Don's brother Steve, the face, along with hotelier Ian Schrager, of New York's fabled Studio 54). Only a small sample of the collection of 1,500 pieces (attached to names such as Damien Hirst, Cindy Sherman and Keith Haring) is on display at a time and rotated regularly. Art historians may want to plumb the 40,000-edition strong research library. Incidentally, this place used to contain swag of a different kind; it was a Drug Enforcement Agency warehouse that served as a halfway house for stacks of money and sacks of pot and coke seized in raids.

Vizcaya Museum *(right)*
& Gardens
3251 S Miami Avenue, Coconut Grove
Tel: 305 250 9133
www.vizcayamuseum.org
Open: 9.30am–4.30pm. Closed Tues, Thanksgiving and Christmas.

Vizcaya is the last thing you would expect to find in Miami; it's just like a stately European home overlooking the water, except the water is Biscayne Bay. Industrialist James Deering built

culture…

171

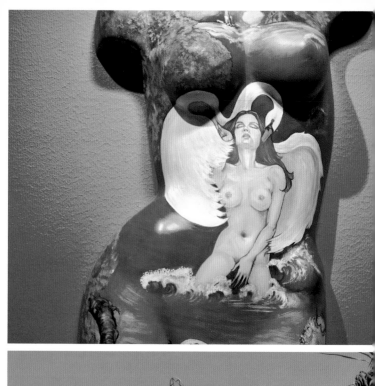

the building in 1916 with Paul Chalfin in charge of the design; it served as his winter home until his death in 1925. The mansion holds 34 rooms decorated with European antiques (dating from the16th- to the 19th-centuries), as well as marble bathrooms, one of the first intercom systems and a pipe organ from 1917. Adjacent to the bay are two gazebos that look out over a magnificent stone barge, which is a petrified Italian sea vessel. The 10-acre grounds are landscaped in the style of Renaissance French and Italian gardens, with cascading pools, fountains and statues peacefully completing the illusion that you are living in a different era. But alas, you're only visiting.

Wolfsonian-FIU
1001 Washington Avenue
(10th St), South Beach
Tel: 305 531 1001
www.wolfsonian.org
Open: noon–6pm (9pm Thurs/Fri).
Closed Weds and holidays. Admission fee.

Wolfsonian-FIU is a small but stunning museum. Practically unique in the U.S., it contains two permanent collections; the largest U.S. display of political propaganda from the two World Wars, including posters, postcards, toys and books; and an impressive collection of items from the modern era in the U.S. and Europe from 1885 to 1945, which concentrates on design and the relationship between man and object. A range of industrial goods and new art forms that heralded the rapid advancement of technology are also on show.

World Erotic Art Museum *(top)*
1205 Washington Avenue
(12th St), South Beach
Tel: 305 532 9336
www.weam.com
Open: 11am–10pm (midnight Fri/Sat). Admission fee.

Miami Beach and naked people would have to be the most natural combination since peanut butter and chocolate. Or not. It wasn't easy, but WEAM was given license to open in 2006 to show the collection of erotic art and artefacts of Naomi Wilzig. The Holocaust survivor grandmother started the journey more than 20 years ago when her son asked her to seek out some 'erotic conversation pieces' for his apartment. Wilzig began amassing the treasures for herself, and the assortment is now valued at more than $10 million (she thinks of herself as an advocate of her chosen niche and its many implications, and has written five books on the subject). The drawings, sculptures, murals and, um, machines from all over Asia and Africa wind their way around 20 rooms (12,000-square-foot of space, in total). If you let them, they can occupy you for several hours (and serve as quite the conversation starter back home). Tours are available; if Ms. Wilzig is in residence, seek her out – she's a hoot.

Ziff Jewish Museum *(bottom)*
301 Washington Avenue
(3rd St), South Beach
Tel: 305 672 5044
www.jewishmuseum.com
Open: daily, 10am–5pm. Closed Mon and Jewish and civil holidays. Admission fee.

culture...

A former 1936 Art Deco-detailed synagogue where Miami Beach's Jewish congregation first met, the building underwent a two-year, $1.5-million restoration before opening as the Ziff Jewish Museum in 1995 (take note of the copper dome and six dozen stained glass windows). The museum evolved from a travelling historic exhibition named MOSAIC, which documented the history of the Jewish community in Florida from 1763 through to the present.

THEATRES

 Actors' Playhouse at the Miracle Theater
280 Miracle Mile (Salzedo), Coral Gables
Tel: 305 444 9293
www.actorsplayhouse.org

The company moved into this classic Art Deco theatre in 1995, seven years after it was established, and launched a $7-million renovation that made the facilities just about shine. Actors' Playhouse has produced more than 100 productions of musicals and dramas (both originals and Broadway/Off-Broadway favourites) and a similar number of children's theatre shows. Previous productions include Oliver!, the 25th Annual Putnam County Spelling Bee and the 39 Steps.

 Bayfront Park Amphitheater
301 N Biscayne Boulevard
(1st St), Downtown
Tel: 305 358 7550
www.bayfrontpark.miami

Set in the centre of Bayfront Park, the 6,500-seat outdoor theatre facility here is among the coolest on the east coast. From certain angles, it even appears that Miami's skyscrapers have paid admission and are enjoying the show (standing, of course). The line-up is a mix of medium-fame touring musical acts, comedians and musical theatre. LiveNation, along with the City of Miami, operates and manages the theatre, which was renovated in 2009 (see ww.livenation.com for event schedules).

 Colony Theater
1040 Lincoln Road
(Lenox Ave), South Beach
Tel: 305 674 1040
www.colonyandbyrontheaters.com

Supposedly, the staff at Colony Theater is fond of referring to the theatre as the 'Beauty Queen', as she is 75-years-old (and doesn't look a day over 20). It no doubt helped that the Colony had a facelift a couple of years ago. The Art Deco gem that opened as a Paramount Pictures movie house presents theatre, music, opera, dance, comedy and film programmes to a house of 430 seats.

 Fillmore Miami Beach at the Jackie Gleason Theater
1700 Washington Avenue
(17th St), South Beach
Tel: 305 673 7300
www.fillmoremb.com

The former Miami Beach Municipal Auditorium became known in the 1950s as a platform for vaudeville acts, comedy and, sometimes, boxing. The stage matured through several reinventions (including one overseen by noted local architect Morris Lapidus), culminating in its reincarnation as the Fillmore Miami Beach in 2007. The room holds 2,700 patrons who come for name-brand live entertainment; Margaret Cho, Flogging Molly and Miami's Kirova Ballet production of The Nutcracker are typical headliners.

shop...

Locals and tourists alike dress to the nines in Miami, which means South Beach, in particular, has become a magnet for all the big names in fashion, as well as some talented up-and-coming designers who are spoiled for choice when it comes to models showing off their revolutionary designs.

Lincoln Road is the epicentre of South Beach consumerist heaven and is packed with cafés and restaurants that sprawl out onto the walkway. It's a purely pedestrian avenue, so a mixture of shoppers, sightseers and locals share what has effectively become the largest catwalk in Miami. In addition to the abundance of restaurants, there are hundreds of independent shops, the majority of which sell womenswear.

The mainstream fashion resides on Collins Avenue. Shops nestle between the boutique hotels of the Art Deco district and the bustle of Lincoln Road is replaced with a quieter and more peaceful ambience. Washington Avenue provides a more eclectic shopping experience. The road has a reputation for its tattoo parlours and novelty shops, but the somewhat incongruous Diesel and Versace add a little luxury to a street that still hasn't quite managed to shake off the hint of desperation that lingers in the air.

For the best shopping experience in South Beach, start by walking up Collins Avenue heading north from Fifth Street (briefly popping over to Washington Avenue) until you find yourself on Lincoln Road, then turn left. If you're a fan of late-night shopping then you're in for a treat. On South Beach, the majority of the shops stay

open until around 11pm, allowing people to linger longer on the beach and still pack in some shopping and a meal.

Downtown Miami does offer a couple of boutique stores, but the majority of the shops here are budget electronic stores. The Miracle Mile in Coral Gables, however, does deserve a visit. Along with some of the best restaurants in Miami, the street and its surroundings boast some brilliant shops in a more tranquil setting. It's more relaxed here, and you don't need to dress up (just in case you've worn out your glad-rags).

The serious label-hunter should head up to the Bal Harbour shops in North Beach, where all the top designer boutiques lie scattered among a bi-level outdoor space. Alternatively, the Village of Merrick Park in Coral Gables is worth a try as the site of countless designer shops that appeal to the area's European sensibilities. What you'll find in these places isn't likely to be cheap – so break out the heavy plastic.

Shopping in Miami is not taken lightly. If you're in a rush, then dash over to one of the malls, but for a real taste of the city, take yourself out for a fashionable stroll on South Beach.

▪ COLLINS AVENUE

Collins Avenue runs for nearly nine miles; from the southern tip of South Beach right up to Bal Harbour's malls and home to some of Miami's most exclusive restaurants and hotels After you've finished your morning's shop, make a pit-stop at Jiminy Cricket Café/bar at the Whitelaw for a cappuccino and a panini.

A/X Armani Exchange
760 Collins Avenue (8th St), South Beach
Tel: 305 531 5900
www.armaniexchange.com

A/X Armani Exchange needs little introduction – especially in Miami, when designer labels are clad to everyone who's anyone. One of many upmarket designer labels in South Beach, A/X Armani Exchange offers smart attire for style-conscious hipsters. Don't expect anything outrageous, just Giorgio's signature wares in a range of subdued, sensible colours. Greys, blacks and whites abound here, with plenty of stock suited to the offiice. Surprisingly, prices are sensible, too, meaning you can splash a little bit more cash on that little black dress.

Banana Republic
800 Collins Avenue (8th St), South Beach
Tel: 305 674 7079
www.bananarepublic.gap.com

Smarter than GAP but with a preppy edge, Banana Republic has Ralph Lauren aspirations without the high price tag. This tastefully designed store is a great place to stock up on summer essentials and winter warmers for a quarter of the price of its European outlets; and with everything made in limited numbers, you can rest easy knowing that it's unlikely you'll rock up somewhere wearing the same thing as someone else. The shame!

Co-op Barney's
832 Collins Avenue (8th St), South Beach
Tel: 305 421 2010
www.barneys.com

There's no need to pound the people-crammed streets of New York for a slice of the pie at Barney's; rummage for designer wares right here on Miami Beach at Co-op Barney's. Trendy, unduly expensive attire for a younger market than the original Barney's; designer clothes, bags, shoes and accessories await in this oversized outlet, with plenty of happy, smiley staff to help you slip into something comfortable. Be sure to bring your plastic – you'll need it.

Club Monaco
624 Collins Avenue (6th St), South Beach
Tel: 305 674 7446
www.clubmonaco.com

High street is given a high-end makeover at Club Monaco, which uses its Miami store to flog its range of super-stylish wares. A clean, fresh take on mail-order classics for men and women; items on offer include clothing, accessories and homeware. Owned by Polo Ralph Lauren, the stock here alternates between a casual collection for spring/summer and more formal attire for autumn/winter; its signature, however, is its classic black and white styles, using only hints of colour when necessary. And with everything made according to European tailoring, you can expert sharp, comfortable looks that really shine.

Guess

736 Collins Avenue (7th St), South Beach
Tel: 305 673 8880
www.guess.com

Bling is the thing at Guess?, which stocks rock star-friendly denim for fashionistas and fame-seekers. Expect bold, adventurous clothes that set trends and grab headlines. Guess? sells everything from clothes and shoes to jewellery and watches at prices significantly lower than in Europe.

Intermix

634 Collins Avenue (6th St), South Beach
Tel: 305 531 5950
www.intermixonline.com

Stocking everything from casual classics to designer finery, Intermix is a, er, mixed bag of gorgeous goodies. Expect hip fashion from the high-end designers and labels that matter; everything from distressed denims to glam evening dresses can be found here, with its Collins Avenue outlet a shrine to high-end design.

Kenneth Cole

190 8th Collins Avenue (8th St), South Beach
Tel: 305 673 5151
www.kennethcole.com

Straightforward American fashion from a straightforward American designer; what more could any style-savvy fashion fan ever want? Kenneth Cole sells clothes, shoes and accessories for both men and women, all with a socially-conscious edge. Guilt-free shopping –who'd have thought it?!

Kidrobot

638 Collins Avenue (7th St), South Beach
Tel: 305 673 5807
www.kidrobot.com

Arty clothes, toys, books and accessories for that special toddler in your life – all with a stylish, designer twist, of course. With everything imported from Japan, Hong Kong and Europe, the stock here is distinctly non-American – and sold in limited numbers, you can be assured that other kids on the playground won't have the same. Occasional artist signings are also organised in-store to launch limited-edition items, so check the website for upcoming events.

Nicole Miller

656 Collins Avenue (7th St), South Beach
Tel: 305 535 2200
www.nicolemiller.com

Gents, watch your credit cards – there'll be no stopping the lady in your life once she's stepped into Nicole Miller. Sassy and sexy clothes designed for beach life; Nicole Miller has got the Miami vibe down to a tee. Her store on Collins Avenue would have even the most restrained shopper reaching for the credit card, with a range of whimsical, creative pieces that truly inspire.

Puma Store

820 Collins Avenue (8th St), South Beach
Tel: 305 674 1407

www.puma.com

Fitness-orientated Miami loves the Puma Store, which stocks an extensive range of style-conscious sportswear. With its image recently revamped, don't dare to step into a style-savvy Miami gym without stocking up here first. In a city where trackie bottoms just aren't an option, the Puma store is a must-shop.

Quiksilver
750 Collins Avenue (8th St), South Beach
Tel: 305 674 9283
www.quiksilver.com

Sun, sand and surf abound in Miami, which is why it makes sense for shaggy-haired surfer dudes to drop by Quiksil-ver for board shots, flip-flops and other accessories. Perfect for that casual 'I-couldn't-care-less' look – even though we all know they do. Surf's up, dude!

Urban Outfitters
653 Collins Avenue (8th St), South Beach
Tel: 305 535 9726
www.urbanoutfitters.com

Low-key but no less stylish, Urban Outfitters has Miami's coolest kids looking sharp whatever the weather. Men's and women's urban apparel and accessories can be found here, all with a designer edge. Quirky accessories for the home finish things off nicely, with an extensive range on offer at the Collins Avenue branch.

LINCOLN ROAD

Lincoln Road is the spiritual home of South Beach – think hip restaurants and smart shops, sprinkled with starlets, lotharios and, of course, tourists. Most likely, you'll be folded into a cosy chair outside Tiramesu cafe, or waiting patiently for a table outside Sushi Samba to sip a mojito and engage in some star-spotting. When you're not, have a wander around Lincoln Road's countless shops.

All Saints Spitalfields
902 Lincoln Road (Jefferson
Ave), South Beach
Tel: 786 517 8180
www.allsaints.com

Ridiculously popular Brit chain All-Saints Spitalfields finally comes to the U.S. in this fabulous outpost on Lincoln Road. The store has become famous thanks to its classic and vintage-look attire for both men and women; it's certainly not cheap, but you pay for the rock 'n' roll edge. Its boots are wildly popular, as are its gothic-tinged accessories. The shop itself is something of a wonder, too, with its signature Singer sewing machines lining the window and dark wooden flooring underfoot.

Affliction
1655 Meridian Avenue (Lincoln
Ln N), South Beach
Tel: 305 538 0095

www.afflictionclothing.com

Get the Miami look at Affliction, where a graphic tee is sure to pack a punch. The store sells tops emblazoned with out-there prints, many of which have become a hit with a-listers across the world; a focus on style and quality means that you get what you pay for with statement pieces that really stand out from the fashion crowd.

Amethyst Couture

1692 Jefferson Avenue (17th St),
South Beach
Tel: 305 673 2801

A fashionista's find; Amethyst Couture has everything a gal needs for a night on the tiles. With everything displayed in a beautiful boutique setting, Amethyst Couture sells clothes, jewellery and everything in between for those packing daddy's credit card. Everything you need to rock the red carpet like the SoBe superstar you are.

Anthropologie

1108 Lincoln Road (Alton
Rd), South Beach
Tel: 305 695 0775
www.anthropologie.com

If you're not inspired by the beautiful items on sale at Anthropologie, then you're beyond help; the stock is simply breathtaking. Boho chic has a home at the Lincoln Road outlet, which sells fashion, accessories and homeware with a vintage, eco edge. Its window displays are pretty damn special, too.

Base

939 Lincoln Road (N Michigan Ave),
South Beach
Tel: 305 531 4982
www.baseworld.com

With everything under one roof, Base in a one-stop credit card-punishing stop. Miscellaneous knick-knacks abound here, including music, books, accessories and clothes for both men and women.

Bebe

1029 Lincoln Road (Lenox Ave),
South Beach
Tel: 305 673 0742
www.bebe.com

If anywhere knows what women want, it's Bebe; its cool clothes are perfect for sultry SoBe nights. Selling fabulously feminine clothing, Bebe is a fashionista's dream come true; expect dresses, tops, shoes, jeans, handbags and accessories spread across a suitably stylish space on Lincoln Road. You're sure to emerge laden with bags.

Christian Audigier

442 Lincoln Road (Washington
Ave), South Beach
Tel: 305 673 5514
www.christianaudigier.com

Bling is the thing at Christian Audigier, the godfather of rock 'n' roll street couture. Indeed, the man behind Ed Hardy and Von Dutch certainly knows what he's doing at his eponymous store on Lincoln Road; stock up on garish, tattoo-inspired trucker caps, hoodies, tees, jeans and board shorts. L.A. style

shop...

181

comes to Miami – and not a moment too soon. Who said flash was trash?

Fly Boutique

650 Lincoln Road (Washington Ave), South Beach
Tel: 305 604 8508
www.flyboutiquevintage.com

Vintage has a home at Fly Boutique; set inside eclectic interiors, you'll find everything from torn jeans to retro suits. The best bit? Everything is displayed as if it was designer, making for a very trendy space indeed. No wonder stylists flock here in their designer-clad droves, searching for something suitably sexy for their clients to slip into.

I Strada

811 Lincoln Road (Meridian Ave), South Beach
Tel: 305 532 1123
www.istradamiami.com

Tired of Miami's flashy fashions? Then check out I Strada, which is all about comfortable, casual clothes for the more sensible Susans among us. Cool, understated female fashion is what you'll find inside; not very Miami at all, but it works. After all, not everyone wants to dress like a hooker hanging out on the corner of Lincoln Road.

Lucky Brand

928 Lincoln Road (N Michigan Ave), South Beach
Tel: 305 532 0201
www.luckybrand.com

If Lucky Brand jeans are good enough for the world's shiniest superstars, then they're certainly good enough for us. Endorsed by celebrities across the globe, Lucky Brand sells 'it' jeans to those who appreciate a good pair of denims. The label's signature four-leaf clover logo is stitched into every pair, with a variety of fits and styles for both men and women.

Original Penguin

925 Lincoln Road (N Michigan Ave), South Beach
Tel: 305 673 0722
www.originalpenguin.com

With so many golf courses in Florida, it makes sense to stock up on argyle-patterned fashion at Original Penguin. Get the edge on the green at the Lincoln Road outlet, where golf is more than a game – it's a lifestyle. Aside from casual clothes, the brand also does smarter attire; think sharp tailored suits, double-breasted jackets and slim-fit trousers for that Don Draper look. Bang on-trend.

Post Blue Jean Co.

836 Lincoln Road (Jefferson Ave), South Beach
Tel: 305 673 2124

Those who appreciate a good pair of jeans head to Post Blue Jean Co., which is a shrine to the denim staple. To some, finding the perfect-fitting jeans is a fantasy - but to those who head here to the Lincoln Road branch, it's a reality. With so many styles and fits in-store for both men and women, you're sure to find a pair that's just right. If not, you might as well give up and go home.

Rainbow

315 Lincoln Road (Washington Ave),
South Beach
Tel: 305 535 0980
www.rainbowshops.com

Children and women first is the general rule of thumb when a ship is sinking, and it's also the case at Rainbow, a store specialising in little people and their stylish mothers. Just because you're a kid, it doesn't mean you don't have an interest in fashion. And nowhere understands this better than Rainbow, which sells stylish children's clothes that won't get them beaten up in the playground. Add to that a women's range of clothing and accesories, and Rainbow is one of the hottest stores to hit in SoBe.

Tuccia di Capri

1630 Pennsylvania Avenue
(Lincoln Lane N), South Beach
Tel: 305 534 5865
www.tucciadicapri.com

Feet aren't generally attractive, unless they're stuffed into a pair of Tuccia di Capri designer sandals. Tuccia di Capri crafts luxurious designer sandals that are seen on the feet of socialities and celebrities across the globe; the perfect way to tread the SoBe sand. Go on – treat your feet.

Victoria's Secret

901 Lincoln Road (Jefferson Ave),
South Beach
Tel: 305 695 1814
www.victoriassecret.com

And we didn't think SoBe's fashionistas could wear much less. Apparently they can, particularly when clad in lacy underthings from Victoria's Secret. Selling deliciously seductive lingerie and accessories, Victoria's Secret proves that sex does indeed sell – and if the Lincoln Road branch is anything to go by, the whole world is buying.

Agora

640 Lincoln Road (Pennsylvania Ave),
South Beach
Tel: 727 895 6419
www.shopagora.com

One-of-a-kind trinkets line the shelves at Agora, where locals rub shoulders with tourists over shelves of offbeat accessories from afar. Customers peruse an interesting mix of imported home accessories imported from Indonesia, China and India. But tourist tat this certainly ain't.

Books & Books

927 Lincoln Road (N Michigan Ave),
South Beach
Tel: 305 532 3222
www.booksandbooks.com

Think you're well read? Think again, as the sheer volume of tomes at the Lincoln Road branch of Books & Books will prove otherwise. It may be a chain, but there's no denying that there's a local feel to the Lincoln Road branch; with everything set out across a warren of dimly-lit rooms, this outpost feels more independent than corporate.

Dog Bar

1684 Jefferson Avenue (Lincoln
Ln N), South Beach

Tel: 305 532 5654
www.dogbar.com

Keep your dog in the manner to which it's undoubtedly become accustomed at Dog Bar, where a dog isn't just a dog; it's a pampered prince/ss. Pooches will certainly be pampered and preened here, catering to man's best friend with a fabulously over-the-top range of chic canine accessories. Favourites include eco-friendly dog bowls and a luxe leather pouch packed with wipes for that yucky business in the park. Paris Hilton, eat your heart out.

Ferrari

19575 Biscayne Boulevard
(Aventura Blvd), South Beach
Tel: 305 692 5288
www.store.ferrari.com

There's only one thing cooler than owning a Ferrari – and that's owning all the goodies that go with it. Be the brand, as they say, and that's certainly the case at the Ferrari store on Biscayne Boulevard; here petrol heads can stock up on a wide range of Ferrari-branded goodies to help them look the part.

Jonathan Adler

1024 Lincoln Road (Lenox Ave),
South Beach
Tel: 305 534 5600
www.jonathanadler.com

As one of America's most popular designers, Jonathan Adler sells everything from bedding through to pottery. His signature use of colour really makes them pop. Clothes may maketh the man, but it is somebody's home that truly speaks volumes about them; to ensure you're not judged on bad taste, stock up on mountains of good taste at Jonathan Adler's store on Lincoln Road.

Peter Lik Gallery

Lincoln Road Mall, 701 Lincoln
Road (Meridian Ave), South Beach
Tel: 786 235 9570
www.peterlik.com

Find magnificent photo landscapes for show and for sale at the Peter Lik Gallery on Lincoln Road. Often described as the single most important landscape photographer alive today, Australia-born Peter Lik shoots vast panoramas that would dazzle even the harshest critic. This gallery is a shrine to his talent, with cool creatives perusing the collection – credit cards at the ready.

Taschen

1111 Lincoln Road (Alton Rd),
South Beach
Tel: 305 538 6185
www.taschen.com

Treasure tomes abound at Taschen, a temple to glossy photo-books and coffee table treasures. With hundreds of gorgeous photo-books displayed in a museum-like setting on Lincoln Road, Taschen is a hedonistic home away from home for anyone who appreciates awe-inspiring aesthetics. Books range from architecture through to fashion, and come in sizes to suit all coffee tables and bookshelves. Those who peruse the tomes are just as hip as the books, pouring over large-format images during their extended lunch hours.

WASHINGTON AVENUE

Collins Avenue's inland neighbour has a slightly grittier edge, with more low-rent stores and a down-to-earth feel. Bodegas and tattoo parlors share the strip with clothiers and a few name brands.

AG Adriano Goldschmied

755 Washington Avenue
(8th St), Miami Beach
Tel: 305 604 7889
www.agjeans.com

Denim is king at AG Adriano Goldschmied, which houses premium jeans in a sleek, sexy setting. Once you go to into the Washington Avenue branch you can't go back; back to any old ordinary pair of jeans, that is. Fitting your legs as if they were custom-made, the denim bought here may be slightly more expensive than what you'd usually fork out, but by God it's worth it.

Belinda's

917 Washington Avenue
(9th St), Miami Beach
Tel: 305 532 0068
www.belindasdesigns.net

Belinda's offers homemade clothing with a hippy, bohemian twist. Boho chic has a home at the Washington Avenue Branch, which specialises in clothes from the 20s and 30s brought bang up-to-date for the 21st-century. Lace, velvet and silk are used for whimsical, floaty dresses that can be worn on the red carpet or on the road.

Dash

815 Washington Avenue
(8th St), Miami Beach

Tel: 305 531 8484
www.kimkardashian.celebuzz.com

Dash needs little introduction; as the boutique belonging to the crazy Kardashian clan, it's had more than enough exposure across hours of reality TV footage. Hollywood starlets Kim, Kourtney and Khloé Kardashian bring their signature style to South Beach at this achingly trendy boutique on Washing Avenue, a black-and-white space filled with designer clothes. Never ones to miss an opportunity to plug themselves, the store also sells Kardashian-branded goodies – such as a not-so subtle water bottle featuring the trio's faces emblazoned across the front.

Deco Collection

901 Washington Avenue
(9th St), Miami Beach
Tel: 305 672 4552

It's all here at Deco Collection, from clothes to music, with everything set against a stark white backdrop. There's a mish-mash of stock, from shoes and sunglasses right through to CDs from local SoBe DJs. According to some, the store also boasts the largest denim collection in South Beach – but you'll have to judge for yourself.

shop...

Diesel

801 Washington Avenue
(8th St), Miami Beach
Tel: 305 535 9655
www.diesel.com

Punish the plastic at Diesel and snap up a pair of the Italian brand's signature jeans. That's exactly what you'll get at this outlet on Washington Avenue, along with accessories and childrenswear. Extremely attractive sales assistants wrap things up nicely – although it can get embarrassing when trying stuff on in too-small dressing rooms.

Passage to India

1143 Washington Avenue
(12th St), Miami Beach
Tel: 305 538 2888

Passage to India sells bohemian trinkets to hippies with an eye for style. In keeping with Washington Avenue's reputation as Miami's slightly more alternative shopping street, here you'll find gifts, accessories and mementos in rich, earthy colours.

The Shop

1121 Washington Avenue
(11th St), Miami Beach
Tel: 305 538 1999

While it's not the most imaginatively-named store in SoBe, the Shop sells incredibly cool designer clothes for both men and women. Upmarket doesn't necessarily mean upped prices, as this Washington Avenue gem proves; its cool collection features brands such as G-Star, True Religion and Diesel.

Star Image

851 Washington Avenue
(9th St), Miami Beach
Tel: 305 673 0851
www.myspace.com/star_image_sobe

So many clothes but nothing to wear? Head to Star Image, which will have you looking like the SoBe superstar you are. Get the ghetto fabulous look at the store on Washington Avenue, where bling is in and glitz is glamour. From baggy hip-hop casuals to red carpet-ready eveningwear, this place will have you looking sharp in no time.

Uncle Sam's Music

1141 Washington Avenue
(12th St), Miami Beach
Tel: 305 532 0973
www.unclesamsmusic.net

DJs stock up on new (and old) tunes at Uncle Sam's Music, where vinyl is God and the customers are nothing but local subjects. Off-duty DJs peruse the racks at Uncle Sam's Music, a store dedicated entirely to new and used vinyl. Categories range from dance right through to hip-hop, so expect a mixed crowd of music-lovers to be queuing at the tills.

MALLS

Aventura Mall

19501 Biscayne Blvd
(Aventura Blvd), Miami Beach
Tel: 305 935 1110
www.aventuramall.com
Open: 10am–9.30pm Mon–
Sat; midday–8pm Sun

The mall makes up more than 2.3-million-square-feet of classic all-American brands (Victoria's Secret, Abercrombie & Fitch, Banana Republic etc.), several department stores including Bloomingdale's, Nordstrom and Macy's, a 24-screen cinema and Coco's Day Spa and Salon. It's a popular destination for families, since organise regular events for children.

Cocowalk
3015 Grand Avenue
(Virginia St), Coconut Grove
Tel: 305 444 0777
www.cocowalk.net
Open: daily, 10am–10pm (11pm Fri/Sat)

Cocowalk is a small, Mediterranean-themed shopping centre that is home to the usual high-street brands. The highlight is that it is outside as opposed to your regular soulless air-conditioned shell. Visiting Brits may like to know that, in addition to those temples of American gastronomy, Chili's and Cheesecake Factory, Cocowalk also harbours a Hooters. Ooh-er!

Dolphin Mall
11401 NW 12th Street
(NW 11th Ave), Miami
Tel: 305 365 7446
www.shopdolphinmall.com
Open: 10am–9.30pm Mon–Sat; 11am–8pm Sun

The Dolphin is a mega-mall with shops, restaurants, cinema and everything else you might expect. Not the most exciting range of stores, but everyone and everything is catered for. Visit its useful website for full shop listings and current sales to decide whether or not the trek is worth it.

Bal Harbour Shops
9700 Collins Avenue
(96th St), North Beach
Tel: 305 866 0311
www.balharbourshops.com
Open: 10am–9pm Mon–Sat; midday–6pm Sun

A high-fashion mecca, the Bal Harbour Shops (and its unique bi-level al fresco shopping experience) consistently outperforms other such malls, hitting a global record of $2,000 a-square-foot in sales in 2008. Naturally, it's home to pretty much every U.S. and European designer one might imagine – all the boys are here, from Armani and Valentino to Dolce & Gabbana, Prada, Custo Barcelona, YSL, Cavalli, and more.

The Village of Merrick Park
358 San Lorenzo Avenue
(Ponce De Leon Blvd), Coral Gables
Tel: 305 529 0200
www.villageofmerrickpark.com
Open: 10am–9pm Mon–Sat; midday–6pm Sun

The Village mall is a hot contender for Bal Harbour's title. Bold-faced names to be found here include Jimmy Choo, Diane von Furstenberg and Loro Piana – in all, an eye-watering list of the crème-de-la-crème of the fashion world. Alleviate post-purchase remorse at the Elemis Spa (see Play).

shop…

play...

If sprawling on the beach or lounging by the pool is too mundane for you, then the good news is that Miami has plenty more to offer. For a city with access to so much water, it is surprising how little people take to watersports – lying on the beach seems to be all that most visitors can manage.

If you do happen to be tempted by surfside activities, they are readily available with jet-skis, kite-boards and surfers competing for the waves. The Miami coastline has acquired a fantastic reputation for scuba-diving, attracting some of the most impressive sea-life in the States. Artificial wrecks have encouraged the spread of coral so shoals of colourful fish, reef sharks and electric eels congregate here in abundance, promising a magnificent underwater experience.

Yachting takes a bit more organisation (and cash). Boat-owners whiz up and down Biscayne Bay comparing engine sizes and oil spills, and you can join them by chartering your own (yacht means 'powerboat' to an American, so be careful to specify whether you want your fuel to be gasoline or wind). The powerboat bug has caught on and the annual Miami Boat Show (in February) is one of the largest events on the city's sporting calendar.

As for airborne thrills, there's parasailing for the daredevils and for the fainter of heart the options range from balloon trips (not very Miami, but certainly a breathtaking experience) to helicopter rides. Skydiving is another popular choice, and while it's uncommon to jump over the water and soar onto the beach, your pilot will ensure that you are suitably scared and guarantee that you have a decent view as you plummet towards the earth.

With so many days of sun, sport fanatics get plenty of practise time. Whether your passion resides on the tennis court or the golf course, Miami has its fair share of clubs to choose from. Golf (with built-in elitist appeal) is unsurprisingly popular in Florida, and whether you're a beginner or a pro, it is a perfect way to spend the day leisurely soaking up the southern sun.

On to the more traditional American sports... Although the Miami Dolphins don't command the same degree of respect that they used to, Florida still remains football country and there's no doubt that Miami loves its pigskin contests, whether they're professional or collegiate in nature. If you happen to be a basketball fan, you should know that the Miami Heat is now regarded as one of the NBA's big-ticket teams. But if you've never taken yourself out to a baseball game, do it now with the Marlins – there are few more enjoyable experiences than a day in the sun at the ballpark listening for the crack of the bat, your thirst quenched by overpriced (but essential) $8 beers.

play...

AMERICAN FOOTBALL

Miami Dolphins

Sun Life Stadium, 2269 Dan
Marino Blvd (NW 199th St)
Tel: 305 623 6100
www.miamidolphins.com

The American Football season takes place from August until February. The Dolphins last reached the playoffs in 2001, but have not won the Super Bowl since 1973. Super Bowl XLIV, in which the feel-good New Orleans Saints defeated the favourite Indianapolis Colts 31-17, was the last big contest to be held in Sun Life Stadium in February 2010.

University of Miami Hurricanes

Sun Life Stadium, 2269 Dan
Marino Blvd (NW 199th St)
Tel: 305 284 3838
www.hurricanesports.cstv.com/sports/
footbl-tickets/mifl-footbl-tickets-body.html

The University of Miami Hurricanes are five-time national champions and winners of the 2004 Orange Bowl. Floridians are, on the whole, more excited to root for the Hurricanes than any of the three home state national teams.

BALLOON RIDES

Miami Ballooning

Meeting point: Holiday Inn Express,
13475 SW 131st St (SW 133rd Ct). Miami
Tel: 305 860 5830
www.miamiballoonrides.com

There is not a great deal of choice when it comes to ballooning. Miami Ballooning dominates the market, offering trips all year round to experience stunning views of South Florida, the Atlantic Ocean and the Florida Everglades. Jeff, Mark or Jean Francois, depending on who is flying your balloon on the day, meet clients at around 6am and flights commence at 6.45am. Flights last 45 minutes to an hour, and it takes 30–40 minutes to get back to the meeting point. All trips even include a post-flight picnic.

BASEBALL

Florida Marlins

Sun Life Stadium, 2269 Dan
Marino Blvd (NW 199th St)
Tel: 305 626 7400
www.florida.marlins.mlb.com

Since the most powerful sluggers and dextrous fielders hail from the Caribbean and Latin America, it's a wonder it took until 1993 to establish a team in Miami. The Marlins won the World Series Championship in 1997 and 2003, and when their new stadium (hopefully) opens in time for the 2012 season, they'll be formally known as the Miami Marlins.

BASKETBALL

American Airlines Arena

601 Biscayne Boulevard (NE
8th St), Downtown Miami
Tel +1 786 777 1000

www.nba.com/heat
Season: October–April

Watch the NBA's Miami representatives play at the American Airlines Arena in Downtown Miami. The Heat, after some high-profile acquisitions, have climbed their way up the popularity list. Tickets range from $10 to $475 and can be hard to come by. If they're sold out, try the Heat Ticket Exchange (link on website) for second market opportunities.

GOLF

Biltmore Golf Course

1210 Anastasia Avenue (Granada Blvd), Coral Gables
Tel: 305 460 5364
www.biltmorehotel.com

The 18-hole course that forms part of the legendary Biltmore Hotel was laid out in 1925 by Donald Ross, a noted course designer and a Scotsman (after all, they did invent the game). Given that this course is known as one of the finest in the South, you might even spot a few famous faces. If your partner doesn't fancy a round, there is always a luxurious spa, a fabulous pool, or the exceptional Fontana restaurant to keep them entertained.

Crandon Golf Course

6700 Crandon Boulevard, Key Biscayne
Tel: 305 361 9129
www.crandongolfclub.com
Open: daily, 7am–6.30pm

The 18-hole links at Crandon Golf Course is one of the best public courses in Florida. Enveloped by the tropics, it features seven saltwater lakes, mangrove thickets, sand traps and several holes that come with Biscayne Bay views, making it a unique and scenic course. The Crandon Golf course is conveniently situated close to South Beach and happens to be the only course with a subtropical lagoon in North America.

Doral Golf Resort & Spa

4400 NW 87th Ave (NW 41st St), Miami
Tel: 305 592 2000
www.doralresort.com

Golf fanatics are never going to go unchallenged at this resort, which opened in 1962 and now forms part of the Marriott family. The Doral has five championship courses totalling 34,000 yards sprawled across its expertly cared-for grounds. With a golf school offering private lessons and group instruction, this course is an ideal place to learn golf as well as watch it (the Doral hosts the PGA Tour).

Miami Beach Golf Club

2301 Alton Road, Miami Beach
Tel: 305 532 3350
www.miamibeachgolfclub.com

Opened in 1923 – and restored to its original lustre with a $10-million brush-up in 2003 – this 18-holer is located in the heart of South Beach on the west side of the island. Designed by Arthur Hills, renowned for his course architecture, the Miami Beach Golf Club was once a training ground for the U.S. Army in World War II. Facilities include a clubhouse with restaurant and expert golf instructors.

MOTORCYCLE RENTALS

Eagle Rider Miami
7871 NW 15th Street, Miami
Tel: 305 468 0108
www.eaglerider.com/miami
Open: daily, 9am–5pm

BMWs, Hondas and Harleys are available to rent on South Beach – even such legendary models as 'Fat Boy' and 'Electra Glide Classic'. Riders must be 21 or over, hold a valid motorcycle driver's licence and a major credit card. Beards and bandanas are optional.

AIR TOURS & HELICOPTERS

PHS
Kendall Tamiami Executive Airport,
14250 SW 129th Street, Miami
Tel: 305 552 8555
www.helicoptersovermiami.com

Locals use this firm to treat their children for achieving good grades at school. You can rise over Miami Beach, Star Island, Brickell and Key Biscayne, until hummers resemble toy cars, choosing from Robinson (R44) helicopters (1 to 3 passengers, 30- or 60-minute tours for $300 or $600, respectively) or Bell 407s (up to 6 people, $900 to $1,800). For total mid-air indulgence, the company offers helicopter service to and from

a local winery (plus tour) from $495.

Miami Flightseeing
North Perry Airport, W
Airport Rd, Hollywood
Tel: 305 767 1903
www.miamiflightseeing.com
Open: daily, 10am–9pm

Pilots in 'high wing' aircraft at Miami Flightseeing take flyers for swooping tours (with commentary) over Miami, South Beach and Biscayne Bay, with special Miami Sunset and Romance options. Flights leave from an airport 30 minutes north of Miami, but the company can arrange a hotel pick-up and drop-off ($90 per couple, plus $35 for each additional person).

JET SKIS

Boucher Brothers
420 Lincoln Road 265 (Washington Ave), Miami Beach
Tel: 305 535 8177
www.boucherbrothers.com

Boucher Brothers is a full-service water-sports company that is in charge of all rentals on Miami Beach, including umbrellas and beach chairs. Look for the blue Boucher Brothers umbrellas to rent a jet ski on the beach. The wave runners are standard class, but powerful enough to give passengers a good dose of adrenaline.

Jet Ski Tours
1655 James Avenue (Lincoln Rd), Miami Beach

Tel: 305 538 7547
www.jetskitoursofmiami.com

Jet Ski Tours operates in Biscayne Bay, and allows clients to drive their Yamaha wave runners right past Star Island – much to the dismay of the resident movie stars and rappers. Allegedly, dolphins and salt-water crocodiles have been spied as well, but unfortunately they're just as camera-shy as the celebs. Jet Ski Tours also conducts boat tours and offers snorkelling packages. Booking advised.

KITE-BOARDING

Miami Kite Boarding
Rickenbacker Causeway, Key Biscayne
Tel: 305 345 9974
www.miamikiteboarding.com

Kite-boarding, or kite-surfing, takes place at Key Biscayne, a 15-minute drive from South Beach. Classes are available for first-timers, and surfers will be taken to sandbars to improve take-offs before splashing into the shallows to cool off with the resident sharks and graceful manta rays.

LIMO TRANSPORT

South Florida Limos
19408 NE 26th Avenue, Miami
Tel: 866 770 1818
www.southfloridalimos.com

There is nothing like a Hummer limo to turn heads in Miami. With fully-stocked bars and entertainment systems inside, there is no real reason to get out of one, unless, of course, you want to go to a nightclub or bar to recruit more limo lovers. Weekend rates start at $125 an hour plus 20 per cent gratuity, with a five-hour minimum. The total increases with the number of stops, so try to do a bit of pre-party planning.

LUXURY CAR RENTALS

There are no two ways about it: boys in Miami believe that flash cars and big wallets impress girls on South Beach. And judging by the number of attractive girls being driven around in Ferraris by greasy, unattractive boys, you'd have to admit that they have a point. So just think how many pretty girls might think you're a superstar if you rent a souped-up Lamborghini for the evening. Some of them might even hop in for a ride. Remember to drive very slowly, rest your left elbow on the open window and rev up the engine to at least 8,000 rpm when driving down Collins Avenue; then turn around and do it all over again.

Dream Exotic
Miami International Airport,
1640 NW 42nd Ave
Tel: 305 235 3369
www.hotcarsmiami.com

Dream Exotic's range of cars does cover the latest high-end convertibles, but should you feel that wheels aren't enough for you it also provides yacht rental and jet charters – just in case you're feeling a little more indulgent.

....

Excellence Luxury Car Rental
Miami International Airport and
3900 NW 25th St, Miami
Tel: 305 526 0000
www.excellenceluxury.com

With a selection that covers luxury cars, exotic convertibles, prestige coupés and SUVs, you're sure to find your perfect rental at Excellence Luxury Car Rental. Its focus is on the latest high-end imports.

....

Exclusive Auto Rental
Miami International Airport,
1640 NW 42nd Ave
Tel: 305 794 2017
www.exclusiveautorental.com

With free delivery and pick-up, Exclusive Auto Rental offers 24-hour reservations and lots of shiny convertibles. And just in case you manage to get lost, all cars come with GPS.

....

PAINTBALL

Ruff N Tuff Paintball
7965 W 2nd Court, Hialeah
Tel: 305 953 7776
www.ruffntuffpaintball.com

The set-up at Ruff N Tuff is extremely professional; it's run by Peter Bofill, who has over 20 years of experience in the game. Clients can shoot at each other on three different battlegrounds; the woods, for the jungle warfare lover; and the Hyperball and the Lego fields for those more partial to guerrilla warfare.

....

PARASAILING

Miami Beach Parasail
behind Loews Hotel, 1601 Collins
Avenue (16th St), Miami Beach
Tel: 305 266 4144
Open: daily, 10am–6pm

Miami Beach Parasail is the only parasailing company on South Beach, and its parachute, 800 feet up in the air, can be seen all along the beach. The captain and his team will send you up in pairs or alone; it's $85 solo for seven to ten minutes, and $150 for a tandem ride of up to 15 minutes. From above, parasailers often see sharks patrolling the Miami coastline and manta rays gliding through the shallow water. The view is spectacular, but the journey out to sea can be a little unnerving when the parachute begins to creak in the wind. Nevertheless, this is an experience not to be missed.

....

SCUBA-DIVING & SNORKELING

Tarpoon Lagoon
300 Alton Road, Miami Beach
Tel: 305 532 1445
www.tarpoondivecenter.com

Ships, subway cars and army tanks have been deliberately sunk along the Miami coast in order to encourage coral growth in the area. The results have been spectacular as divers around the world come to get a glimpse of eagle-rays, nurse sharks, green and spotted moray eels and barracuda. Beginners can take a three-day dive certification course ($349) before attempting their first office drop in the ocean (there's also a one-day Discover program for $199, among others, and equipment is available for rental). Tarpoon organises both daytime and nocturnal dives; Monty's Bar (see Drink) is located beside the shop.

SKY-DIVING

Sky Dive Miami
28730 SW 217th Avenue (SW
292nd St), Homestead
Tel: 305 759 3483
www.skydivemiami.com

Sky Dive Miami jumps with over a thousand first-timers every year. Depending on whether you've chosen basic, deluxe or extreme tandem, you'll be jumping from between 8,000 and 13,500 feet, and can experience a terrifying 20-, 40- or 60-second free-fall, too. A half-hour pre-jump training session is provided, and you can be filmed on request.

SPAS

Canyon Ranch Hotel & Spa
6801 Collins Avenue, North Beach

Tel: 305 514 7000
www.canyonranchmiamibeach.com
Open: daily, 6am–9pm

One of the most prestigious names in luxury spa experiences in the U.S. is Canyon Ranch, and this property – at 70,000-square-feet – is the largest in Florida. The Aquavana thermal spa section includes a Finnish sauna, crystal steam room and ice igloo, while the David Rockwell-blueprinted treatment rooms (all 54 of them) are appropriately stylish and relaxing. A visit here can have you layered in mud, salt or seaweed, or encased in a full body cocoon.

Elemis Spa
330 Avenue San Lorenzo,
2345 Village of Merrick Park (S
Le Jeune Rd), Coral Gables
Tel: 305 774 7171
www.elemis.com/usa/miami.html
Open: daily, 10am–9pm (6pm Sun)

This outpost of the Brit-based Elemis spa brand goes all-out on its facials. The spa offers the usual roster of massages as well, but adds a twist with sessions focused on acupuncture, reflexology and cupping. Perhaps the most attractive option is the Lovers' Ritual, which includes massage classes for lovers before the pampering sessions begin.

Mandarin Oriental Hotel
500 Brickell Key Drive, Downtown
Tel: 305 913 8332 www.
mandarinoriental.com/miami/spa
Open: daily, 9.30am–9.30pm

play...

The Mandarin Oriental's award-winning spa is a tri-level sanctuary that features 17 treatment rooms (six of which overlook Biscayne Bay), a fitness centre and a yoga room. Signature treatments include the Ayurvedic holistic body treatment, Life Dance, Balinese synchronised massage, Thai massage, the Mandarin hot stone therapy and the luxury facial. You may also want to try out the Oriental Harmony, a four-handed(!) soak, scrub and massage.

Ritz-Carlton South Beach

1 Lincoln Road (Collins Ave),
Miami Beach
Tel: 786 276 4090
www.ritzcarlton.com
Open: daily, 9am–8pm (6pm Sun)

The Ritz Carlton's spa covers 16,000-square-feet with no less than 14 calming treatment rooms. The spa's signature treatments include Night Out On the Town (mini facial, express mani/pedi, shampoo/style and makeup), and, presumably for the next day, the SoBe Detox. The entire line of treatments incorporates Carita beauty products. One of the facilities' most popular sessions is the SPAshiatsu, a deep compression/acupressure treatment in which the therapist is suspended from bamboo bars and walks over the client's back. The Ritz-Carlton also offers specialised options designed for men and teens.

The Spa at the Setai

2001 Collins Avenue (20th St),
Miami Beach
Tel: 305 520 6900

www.setai.com/thespa
Open: daily, 9am–9pm

Traditions of the Pacific Rim are referenced by the Setai in its menu of holistic offerings. The Setai's spa is smaller and more personal than its competitors, and is situated in a two-tiered building beside the pool area. Massage treatments include a Himalayan hot stone massage and Balinese massage; wet options include several 'romantic bathing ceremonies' ($75 for 30 minutes), and other signature bath rituals such as the China Sea uplifting bath and the Malaysian Rainforest relaxing bath.

The Standard

40 Island Avenue (Farrey Ln),
Miami Beach
Tel: 305 673 1717
www.standardhotel.com
Open: daily, 8am–10pm
(midnight Fri/Sat)

The Standard Hotel's entire property is based around the spa, which draws influence from world cultures that define 'bathing' as a social practice. Hence the Turkish-style Hammam and scrub room, the Roman waterfall hot-tub, Arctic plunge pool, aromatherapy steam room and cedar sauna. Mud baths, spa treatment rooms, a skincare clinic, holistic massage therapies, yoga classes and herbal and holistic baths of various temperatures and humidities (from $30) render this the ultimate health retreat. Following a wholesome meal at the Standard's restaurant, you'll quickly forget your evening plans in favour of relaxing in blissful peace beside the garden Fire Lounge.

SURFING

Although Hawaii and the States' West Coast are recognised as the true surfing meccas, Florida is long boarder central on the East. Miami Beach can hang with the best of them, but the more impressive spots are found further up the Florida coast.

Florida Surf Lessons

(sessions take place on the beach at 1st and Ocean)
Tel: 561 625 5375
www.floridasurflessons.com

The instructors at Florida Surf Lessons have over 50 years of surfing experience between them, and are trained in CPR, first-aid and water safety. Grab a gang – the price per person decreases as the number of students increases – and prepare to hit the water dozens of times before you can show your face on the same sand as Kelly Slater. There are a number of clinics and workshops held regularly, and board rental is included in the price.

TENNIS

The two-week annual Sony Ericsson Open (starting mid-March) is one of the biggest non-Grand Slam events in the world. Otherwise tennis courts are few and far between on South Beach, but there are several on the Miami mainland, usually situated in private clubs.

Biltmore Tennis

1210 Anastasia Avenue (Columbus),
Coral Gables
Tel: 305 460 5360
www.biltmorehotel.com

Biltmore Tennis is part of the enormous Biltmore Hotel complex. While you get sweaty with the tennis pro you can always send your partner off for a round of golf and reconvene for a delicious lunch by the hotel pool.

Brickell Tennis Club

601 South Miami Avenue
(SE 7th St), Brickell
Tel: 305 375 9122
www.cliffdrysdale.com/brickell

Courts at the state-of-the-art Brickell Tennis Club can only be reserved by members. However, 90-minute clinics ($45) and lessons ($100) are on offer to the public. With typical efficiency, attendants are on-hand to offer fresh towels and cold drinks.

Crandon Park Tennis Center

7300 Crandon Boulevard, Key Biscayne
Tel: 305 365 2300
www.miami-dade.gov/parks/
parks/crandon_tennis.asp
Open: daily, 8am–9pm (7pm Sat/Sun)

Home to the two-week Sony Ericsson Open (starting mid-March), Crandon Park Tennis Center is a beautiful stadium court that shows 13,000 spectators exactly how it's done. For mere mortals, the facility also has 26 courts (hard and clay) and ridiculously reasonable rates.

Flamingo Park Tennis Center

1245 Michigan Avenue (12th St), Miami Beach
Tel: 305 673 7761
Open: 8am–1pm and 3–9pm Mon–Fri, 8am–7pm Sat, Sun

Flamingo Park Tennis Center is found in the centre of Miami Beach and is overseen by GSI Bollettieri, a management company and international tennis-teaching academy. You'll find 19 clay courts (most lighted for night play), a locker room and pro shop. Additional facilities include basketball and baseball courts and a water playground for kids.

YACHT CHARTERS

Powerboats are very popular in Miami. In fact, many Miami locals say that their powerboats are more indicative of their personality than their cars. The bay is popular for cruising, but a trip along South Beach is always tempting, and is a good option for re-enacting that Baywatch-style water rescue.

Florida Yacht

390 Alton Road (5th St), Suite 3, Miami Beach
Tel: 305 532 8600
www.floridayacht.com

What better way to savour the sea than by playing sailor for the week? Crafts can be rented for between $2,600 and $6,000 in value season per week and $3,100 to $7,500 in high season. Rentals range from smaller two-cabin Sundancers to the larger four-cabin Ornana 44 catamarans with 110-foot sail area.

info...

CLIMATE

Generally, the climate in Miami only varies slightly and remains constantly warm. From December to February, Miami's high season, the average daily temperatures range from 16°C to 24°C (60°F to 75°F). The average daily temperature during the North American summer months hovers around 28°C (82°F). Miami's not quite an inferno, though. A cool ocean breeze often helps lower the temperature a bit and gives the beach a refreshing edge; off the beach, shops and eateries entice shoppers with frigid blasts of air. Do remember to use sun block at all times; due to Miami's latitude, the sun's tanning (and burning) effects are much stronger than you might think. Crispy is not a good look.

DRESS

If you want to look the part, it's time to fish your best garments out of the back of your wardrobe. The phrase 'cutting-edge fashion with a slutty *edge*' approximates how people dress in Miami. Jeans are allowed if they are ripped in the right places, but long dresses are unheard of, and trainers or sneakers are not welcome unless you are famous or they really do go with your outfit (odds are, they don't). Wearing a jacket may or may not help men to get into lounges.

DRUGS

Miami has a reputation for being the pharmacy of the south for party-lovers, but drugs are frowned upon and the consumption or distribution of narcotics is strictly prohibited. Undercover cops observe from the shadows, particularly in the more high-profile clubs, and on early Saturday and Sunday mornings when the clubs shut Washington Avenue is jammed with police investigating vehicles. In terms of being offered drugs, in lounge bars you will most likely not encounter anything other than alcohol, but in large downtown clubs drugs may well be on offer. Ladies; be extremely careful with who buys your drinks and keep a close eye on your glass at all times - there have been reports of Rohypnol poisoning (commonly known as the 'date-rape' drug) and the colourless, tasteless substance makes it impossible to detect.

GETTING IN

The Miami bouncer holds the key to the party, so be nice to him, but not so nice so that he thinks you're soft. His criteria are primarily money and good looks, but neither is very effective without self-confidence and a hint of arrogance. If you're a guy and you don't have any hotshot contacts, look the part or arrive flanked by long-legged blondes and have your concierge add your name to the guest list. Arrive early and look your best, otherwise the velvet ropes will not be lowered for you – ever. For ladies, it is much less problematic to show up at the top parties, since a gang of girls at a club attracts more girls (and more men to turn away at the door).

PARKING

If you're unfortunate enough to have chosen a hotel without airport pickup, or have aspirations larger than a three-block radius, you may well be renting a car. That means you'll have to deal with the scourge of parking. A word of warning; finding a spot on the street is nearly impossible in South Beach on weekend nights, as residents trawl in from the suburbs to entertain themselves, and the garages change their payment method to flat-rate entry. In general, the major indoor garages, including the ones on 16th Street and 13th Street (both just off Collins), are safe and secure, and spots are readily available. Rates run about a dollar an hour. On the street the rate is $1.50 per hour (in most cases). Just estimate how long you'll be, pay (the meter machine takes change or credit), and place the strip that's emitted inside the car on the driver's side dash. Parking is free from 3 to 9am - presumably officials think that everyone is impaired during that period and it's for the best to leave them be.

SMOKING

Smoking is banned in all restaurants, but it is permitted in freestanding bars where food sales are not a significant percentage of revenue. There are no formal regulations when it comes to hotels, but many properties do have their own 'no smoking' policies. It's best to ask on check-in, as fines for lighting up are steep.

TAXIS

Miami cabs make New York taxis look cheap. The dire public transport system in the city means that if you haven't rented a car taking a cab is the only option. Taxi firms are well aware of this and the cabs' fare meters move faster than the second hand of a clock. A taxi from the airport to Downtown is roughly $22; to the Lincoln Road area of South Beach is a $32 flat fare; a taxi from South Beach to Downtown runs about $15.

TIPPING

The cost of your holiday just went up by 20 per cent. Waiters, waitresses and bartenders don't earn a proper wage, so they rely on tips as their sole source of income. Tipping, therefore, is a must. In Miami you are supposed to tip in taxis, bars, nightclubs and even when you dry your hands in the 'restroom' – basically, at every opportunity. On South Beach it is common for the bill to have an extra 18 per cent added onto it for service, forcing patrons from parts unknown to pay a gratuity because Europeans are notorious for shirking their tipping responsibilities. You can, however, pay a reduced amount (for the tip, not the bill) if you think the service is not up to scratch. In bars, be sure to tip after every drink you buy; usually $1 or $2 per drink is adequate and will ensure efficient service. Bartenders will overlook you if the tips dry up.

index...

Hedonism /hedoniz'm/
'The philosophy that pleasure is the highest
good and proper aim of human life.'
– Oxford English Dictionary

Hg2 Corporate

Branded Gifts....

Looking for a corporate gift with real value? Want to reinforce your company's presence at a conference or event? We can provide you with branded guides so recipients will explore their chosen city with your company's logo right under their nose.

Branding can go from a small logo discreetly embossed on to our standard cover, to a fully custom jacket in your company's colours and in a material of your choice. We can also include a letter from your CEO/Chairman/President and add or remove as much or as little other content as you require. We can create a smaller, 'best of' guide, branded with your company's livery in a format of your choice. Custom guides can also be researched and created from scratch to any destination not yet on our list.

For more information, please contact Tremayne at tremayne@hg2.com

Content licensing....

We can also populate your own website or other materials with our in-depth content, superb imagery and insider knowledge.

For more information, please contact Tremayne at tremayne@hg2.com

Hg-Who?

Welcome to the world of Hg2 – the UK's leading luxury city guide series. Launched in 2004 as the *A Hedonist's guide to…* series, we are pleased to announce a new look to our guides, now called simply Hg2. In response to customer feedback, the new Hg2 is 25% lighter, even more luxurious to look at or touch, and flexible, for greater portability. However, fear not, our content is still as meticulously researched and well-illustrated as ever and the spirit of hedonism still infuses our work. Our brand of hedonism taps into the spirit of 'Whatever Works for You' – from chic boutique hotels to well-kept-secret restaurants, to the very best cup of coffee in town. We do not mindlessly seek out the most expensive; instead, we search high and low for the very best each city has to offer.

So take Hg2 as your companion to a city. Written by well-regarded journalists and constantly updated online at www.Hg2.com (register this guide to get one year of free access), it will help you Sleep, Eat, Drink, Shop, Party and Play like a sophisticated local.

"Hg2 is about foreign life as art" **Vanity Fair**
"The new travel must-haves" **Daily Telegraph**
"Insight into what's really going on" **Tatler**
"A minor bible" **New York Times**
"Excellent guides for stylish travellers" **Harper's Bazaar**
"Discerning travellers, rejoice!" **Condé Nast Traveller**